Essays in Persuasion

On Seventeenth-Century English Literature

Frank Livingstone Huntley

The University of Chicago Press
Chicago and London

FRANK LIVINGSTONE HUNTLEY, emeritus professor
of English at the University of Michigan, is the
author of *Sir Thomas Browne: A Biographical and
Critical Study*, *Dryden's Essay of Dramatic Poesy*,
Jeremy Taylor and the Great Rebellion, and *Bishop
Joseph Hall: A Biographical and Critical Study*.

THE UNIVERSITY OF CHICAGO PRESS, CHICAGO 60637
THE UNIVERSITY OF CHICAGO PRESS, LTD., LONDON

©1981 by The University of Chicago
All rights reserved. Published 1981
Printed in the United States of America

85 84 83 82 81   5 4 3 2 1

LIBRARY OF CONGRESS CATALOGING IN PUBLICATION DATA

Huntley, Frank Livingstone, 1902–
    Essays in persuasion.

    Includes bibliographical references and index.
    1. English literature—Early modern, 1500–1700—
History and criticism—Addresses, essays, lectures.
I. Title.
PR433.H8   1981   820'.9'004   80–14477
ISBN 0–226–36088–1

In grateful memory of two mentors at the
University of Chicago during the mid-1930s
R. S. Crane
and
George Williamson

Contents

Preface

I like the word "essay" because from its French source it means "trial," "testing." In Montaigne as in Locke, an essay can never give us an absolute proof that a particular proposition is true; it merely probes, tosses ideas around, uses fact where it fits, and hopes to convince that the proposition may, after all, be true. Hence the writing of an essay is an art, not a science.

Essays like the ones that follow often begin accidentally while one is searching for something else. These ideas I call "white rabbits," and although pursuing them is fun it can also be dangerous because the major opus gets laid aside while you fall pell mell down the hole with the rabbit twitching his tail just below you. Every one of us at some time or other has had a hunch, an idea, a hypothesis that at first seemed ridiculous and then too obvious. Why not pursue it?

I did have to abandon one a long time ago. Wondering about a motive for Dr. Thomas Browne's strange silence on the loss of his favorite son Thomas at sea while serving in the English navy, I became convinced that it was family shame: the lad, like Billy Budd, had been court-martialed and hanged from the yardarm. So many hours and days passed by in the Public Record Office and the Admiralty files that I almost forgot that research on Jeremy Taylor had initially brought me to London. That "white rabbit" ended nowhere, but on the way down I tasted some delicious concoctions stored in jars within easy reach on the various shelves. There is no relationship between time spent and the result.

Occasionally we find material that seems worth building into something. Literary problems like canonicity, or dating, or background, or transcription, or any other, all require rhetoric. Take a piece of unknown authorship, for example. There is usually a reason for anonymity, and the more compelling the reason the greater the effort at the time to conceal the identity of the author. Since, with the passage of history, direct evidence is unlikely to appear, the procedure can only be one of persuasion resting on probability, an argument that joins relevant parts of the poem or play to historical facts that lie outside. As in all circumstantial cases, such arguments inevitably produce counterarguments. And yet, in the process that may last years, as weaker arguments give way to stronger, a preliminary "hunch" may turn into, and often has become, an accepted "fact." What else is literary and historical criticism," asks Matthew Arnold in *God and the Bible*, "but a series of most delicate judgements on the data given us by research—judgements requiring great tact, moderation, and temper?"

Throughout Western civilization such elegant structures have been raised by rhetoric. Our responsibility, by mastering their means of knowing and their method of demonstration, is continually to bring to the present, through our arguments, a better understanding of the past.

A wise and dear scholarly friend of mine, Dr. Walter Pagel, M.D., medical historian, told me years ago that whenever he came across some good "material" he used it at least three times. All but three of the following essays in persuasion have appeared before, some as an article, others in a book, still others as an article collected by some one else in a book. But I never use the same material a fourth time; that is too many. The older essays have been, for the most part, rigorously rewritten, ruthlessly shortened, where appropriate brought up-to-date, and , I hope, thus made more persuasive. Their subjects follow roughly a chronological order.

The first essay and the last, merely autobiographical, do not intend to "persuade" anybody to anything. The first may show how I became so used to religion as a child as to be drawn almost inevitably toward the seventeenth century and the language of the King James Bible. The last may illustrate the kind of life we scholars love and cannot cling to forever any more than other people can cling to theirs, another seventeenth-century motif.

I am grateful to the editors and directors of the following journals and publishing houses who originally and daringly sponsored most of the material in this book: the *Anglican Theological Review*, D. S. Brewer, Ltd., *English Literary History*, *Essays in Literature*, Midwest Modern Language Association, *Modern Language Notes*, *Modern Philology*, *Publications of the Modern Language Association*, *Philological Quarterly*, *Review of English Studies*, *Studies in the Literary Imagination*, the University of Michigan Press, and the *University of Toronto Quarterly*.

To my parents, my former teachers, my wife, Katharine, my children, fellow scholars, dear friends, and of course to Providence I owe the deepest gratitude.

Beginnings: On Being
a Missionary Kid

I was born in China and live in the United States; started out as a British subject and became an American citizen; was raised as a Baptist and long ago turned Anglican.

When the Communists took over China (Chiang Kai-shek and his Nationalists having failed the revolution), there were in that country several thousand Protestant Christian missionaries, most of whom had large families, possibly as a bulwark against cultural isolation. Hence there must be even more thousands of us "missionary kids" around, many in professional life—doctors, preachers, State Department officials, university and college teachers, and, I imagine, some second- and third-generation missionaries in other parts of the globe.

Of the seven children in our family all but the first were born at the Baptist Medical Mission in Hanyang, Hupeh, central China. We were the only foreigners in a city of half a million people. I came along on 10 October 1902, the symmetrical middle: a girl and two boys older than I—Eva, Ralph, and Rex; and a girl and two boys younger—Gladys, Wilfred, and Leslie. Father was obstetrician, physician, dentist, and disciplinarian. Mother was teacher, homemaker, and consoler.

Hanyang is on the south side of the River Han where it flows into the Yangtze. Across the Han is Hankow, and across the Yangtze from these two cities is Wuchang. Today the three cities together are called Wuhan, and a fine bridge connects them, but

Adapted with permission from the *Michigan Quarterly Review* 18 (1979): 72–95.

there was no bridge in my day. One time the Chinese woman rowing us across (they push their oars and face the direction they are going in) was in obvious distress. She fell to the bottom of the boat. Covering her with his raincoat, Father told us to look the other way. Pretty soon we heard a baby crying. Father had helped the woman give birth, and that made us very happy. It was a nice round fat little Chinese boy baby. She wrapped it up, laid it at her feet, and rowed us the rest of the way to Hankow-side, only about half a mile.

In Hanyang brothers Ralph, Rex, and I formed a gang which we called (ungrammatically) "Us Three Boys." I, being the youngest, had to fetch things from the house and run other errands. One day we planned an underground house. How solve the problem of lighting its interior? Ralph the brain hit on using a kerosene oil lantern, several of which were hanging in the utility shed behind Father's hospital. Rex thought that a splendid idea and nominated me to ask Father for it. To our surprise Father called the "boy" to fill one with kerosene (which had been shipped to China for our benefit by the Standard Oil Company). With the unlit lantern beside us we started to dig in an unused portion of the large compound. We dug with a couple of trowels, a kitchen knife, and some old tablespoons the cook grudgingly lent us. The house was to be six feet square and six feet deep. After two full days of digging we had penetrated China's good earth to the depth of about one inch, so we gave up the whole project. Father thought we had put the cart before the horse or else light before darkness.

Since our compound was surrounded by a high wall with broken glass bottles sticking from its cemented top, all our amusements were close at hand—pets, for instance, rabbits, frogs, mice, snakes, and a marvelous shaggy little Chinese donkey. One day Ralph decreed that he should ride first. Rex argued against this plan, while I held the donkey's bridle. But Ralph won and mounted the beast, whereupon Rex picked up a stick and poked the donkey in the ribs. I was knocked backwards, and with a whoop Ralph and the donkey went off at full speed straight toward the orchard. The donkey aimed at the tree with the lowest branches, and in two seconds Ralph lay moaning on the ground and the donkey was eating grass. Rex got spanked for that.

Outdoors we had swings and rings and parallel bars. The iron rings, five of them, hung at the end of long ropes about ten feet apart so that we could travel back and forth like monkeys from one ring to the next. Amah (the nursemaid in charge of children is always Amah) was at one of the rings teaching Gladys, aged three or so, how to hang on by her hands. I was fooling around with the ring next to them. For no reason at all I swung it as hard as I could, and it went sailing this way and that, around and back, and finally hit poor Amah right in the eye. She was writhing on the ground, blood spurting from her forehead. Gladys was yelling because she had been left hanging in the air, and I was bawling from guilt and fright. I thought I had killed Amah, whom we loved very much. She taught us Chinese nursery songs illustrated with the fingers. One was about five little ants who wouldn't come out of their ant-hill. At the end, *"Yi, er, san, sze, ooh, ching nee pow chu lai"*- one, two, three, four, five, won't you please come out? Another song went *"sange buh ma manman tso"*—three white horses going slowly, three little girls walking hand in hand, two boys fighting and screaming, while under the bed the smallest child eats the burnt rice off the edge of the cooking pot. Lucky for us that Father was in his hospital fifty yards away. The cook came running out and carried Amah there. Father gave her chloroform and sewed up the cut. Every time I kissed Father goodnight I could smell chloroform in his clothes and moustache, a nice clean hospitally kind of smell.

Mother had dark hair done up in a bun, and a slim waist. She always seemed to be dressed in a long black skirt that stuck out behind in ruffles and a white shirtwaist that bulged in front. With a bunch of keys at her belt, right after breakfast she opened various cupboards and laid out the clothes, staples, silverware, and everything else the family needed that day. On Saturday mornings Mother and the cook would go over the week's kitchen account. On his big abacus and Mother's little one together they would argue over the cost of this and that, clicking away at their beads down to the last "cash." A cash is a small copper coin with a square hole in the middle.

On Sundays in Hanyang we all went to the chapel in the city outside our compound. The service was conducted by a Chinese pastor whom Father had converted, and during the hymns Mother would pedal the little Estey organ. After church we were allowed to play only Sunday games. We could play "authors," and although I knew that Longfellow wrote "Evangeline" and Whittier, "Snowbound," to this day I cannot tell the nineteenth-century American poets apart because they all looked exactly alike. After years of arguing, Mother allowed us to play "Flinch" on

Sunday if we were quiet about it. But most of Sunday was spent playing "search the Scriptures." This began with each of us reciting our verse, for we had to memorize one verse from the Bible (no fair taking "Jesus wept") and recite it to Mother on Sunday. Then she would announce the lesson for the day, which we would read silently. "Now," she would say, "take your paper and pencils and without looking see how many of the sons of Jacob you can write down." The following Sunday might require us to trace a map of ancient Palestine and put in the twelve tribes where they belonged.

Each morning at the breakfast table before we could touch any food, the family read a whole chapter of the Bible, from Genesis to Revelation (Psalm 119 took several days), each person reading out loud from his own Bible one verse around and around the table. When I was five I acquired my first quadrisyllable, the word "circumcision." I did not understand it, but thereafter I would count the people around the table and read ahead in the chapter, hoping that my verse would have "circumcision" in it. Often some other person got to be the lucky one. It was Mother who taught all seven of us how to read and write.

The rest of Sunday was spent drawing and reading. Any kind of drawing and painting with watercolors was considered suitable for Sunday. No coloring books in those days; we made our own designs. There were special books for Sunday reading. No adventure stories by G. A. Henty or R. M. Ballentyne, but *Robinson Crusoe* and *The Swiss Family Robinson* and all books by Dickens were declared to be fit for Sunday reading, although some of Dickens's novels are pretty bloody as far as I am concerned. We liked Sunday because after church the servants had the day off, and Mother spent all of her time with us.

Three weeks before Christmas Father always made candy on a little spirit stove in his study, enough candy to last the year because we were not allowed to eat anything sold by vendors just outside our gate. Meanwhile Mother would mix Christmas pudding in the largest basin she could find, which was usually the baby's bathtub, scalded of course. She would make balls of plum pudding, tie them up in white cloth, and hang them from the rafters in the attic to drip. Then Father would invite us one by one into his study. There on a table were set out all the toys our parents had ordered from Monkey Wards the previous August. (Not for years did I realize that there was a Montgomery Ward and Company). Each of us would choose one present for each sibling. Father would label them "To Rex from Eva" and so on down the line, putting each present aside as it was chosen.

Every Christmas was different and meant weeks of preparation with all the children helping. Most memorable was "Christmas in the tropics." Father collected all the magic-lantern slides of wild animals that he had and projected each animal to approximately lifesize on large sheets of paper pinned to the study wall. He put me in charge of drawing the outline of the animal with a thick black pencil. I stuck in the eyes where they belonged. Then he gave these sheets of paper to a Chinese carpenter, who cut them out of very thin wood like our quarter-inch plywood today. These he nailed onto larger thick pieces of wood so that the animals would stand up. Then these flat wooden animals were given to a Chinese artist who painted them in the gaudiest colors he could think of. His tiger looked as if it had taken a bath in a rainbow, but all of them were brave and beautiful and some a bit scary. The elephant was the only three-dimensional animal. His body, made of a bamboo-strip frame covered with thick paper painted gray, was about eight feet long and five feet in diameter. He had a wonderful head and ears and trunk. His front and back legs were made of cloth, like two pairs of baggy trousers. Rex was the front legs and I was the back legs. I had to wave the elephant's tail from inside and follow Rex because I could not see out. Rex had to wave the trunk and ears, and both of us occasionally made a trumpeting noise like an elephant. Between us was stretched a hammock full of the wrapped and labeled parcels. Ralph, the elephant keeper, led us around among homemade coconut palms and asked us why we were making such a row. Rex, in his best elephant voice acquired at rehearsal, said that he had a toothache. Ralph peered into the elephant's mouth and said, "My, that looks bad. It had better come out." Rex would place a parcel in Ralph's hand, and as Ralph jerked it out the elephant would squeal with pretended pain.

I was told that in order to get their work done missionaries had to spend at least two of the hot months each year in the mountains or by the seashore. From Hanyang the whole family would go by ricksha, sampan, and train as far as we could toward Kuling. When we got to the bottom of the mountains, Father would argue with the Chinese porters who crowded around to get jobs carrying this large family and all those pieces of luggage. The men would shout and jostle, and Father would scold them in very loud Chinese. We had a dozen trunks made of pigskin, and half a dozen *corries* (bottom and top of flexible rattan that squashed together to hold practically anything) and a dozen *pookai* (bundles of bedding wrapped in yellow oilpaper and tied with rope). The men would heft a large box, pretending that it was much heavier than it was, and scream out, "This is a four-man carry," and Father would yell back, "Nonsense, that's a two-man carry," and the men would say, "Have mercy, make it a three-man carry." It always ended with two men slinging it between them on a bamboo pole. Then came the sedan chair carriers, and the same argument would ensue. Father would want to put Glady's and Wilfred in one chair and Frank and somebody else in another, but the men would grumble, "No, no, he's too fat, he ought to have a chair by himself." Father always won.

At last the journey up the mountain would begin, a long procession. First Mother, under a pink English-made parasol; then the children; then a long line of coolies carrying the impedimenta; and Father in the rear to see that no one ran off with the baggage or dumped a child. We all wore pith helmets. I leaned back, lulled by the gentle swinging of the chair on its bamboo poles, listening to the groans and grunts of the men as occasionally they shifted a pole to the other shoulder, or wiped the sweat off their strong brown backs gleaming in the sun. Far off came the sound of a waterfall, louder and louder, and then fainter and fainter, and I was almost asleep. Then I woke up to a nightingale singing its heart out in a dense grove of bamboo. The sun had gone down without my knowing it. At Kiukiang Father had bought each of us a small sealed jar of gingerroot boiled in thick sweet syrup. Kiukiang is famous for ginger. I opened my jar and ate some.

And finally our Kuling house, high up there on top of a flat rock. Lots of other missionaries and their children had already arrived, and next day we ran around renewing friendships made the summer before. Then crowds of children and grownups would be at the community swimming pool, fed by that stream whose fall I had heard as we came up the mountain. Father taught each of us how to swim at the age of five by throwing us head first off the diving board into deep water. He said that everyone in a family that travels by steamship as much as we do must learn how to swim. We would come up sputtering and begin to dog-paddle.

Church services at Kuling were in English, and all the missionary families sat under the trees in a large circle. And we sang hymns in harmony—none of that off-key Chinese unison we were used to in Hanyang. One of our favorites was "Bringing in the Sheaves," only, instead of the real words, the missionaries sang, "Bringing in Chinese, bringing in Chinese. We shall come rejoicing, bringing in Chinese." Father was tenor in the Kuling Missionary Summer Quartet, and played the autoharp. His self-accompanied masterpiece was "Peace be still," and when he came to "The winds and the waves obey thy will," he stroked the strings louder and louder until we imagined ourselves about to the shipwrecked. My childhood was filled with hymns, many of the words overflowing with fountains of blood.

The familial demiparadise protected from a populous Chinese city by a jagged-glass-topped brick wall was bound to come to an end. The revolution started in our backyard on 10 October 1911. Rex and I were in our attic, building a house of empty Monkey Ward packing cases. "Come here, quick," shouted Rex, at the attic window. "Wuchang's on fire." Sure enough, across the Yangtze River the great round tanks of the Standard Oil Company were sending clouds of black smoke high into the air. Behind us we heard small bangs, and rushing to the other side of the attic we saw a long line of cannon on the ridge of Tortoise Hill. Later Father told us they were French seventy-fives. They were firing their shells over our heads smack into the oil tanks three miles away. Behind Tortoise Hill were the huge Hanyang Iron Works, including the arsenal. Hanyang used to be called the Pittsburgh of China. That is why Sun Yat-sen chose to start his revolution in my hometown.

Father had a picture of Sun Yat-sen in his study. Dr. Sun had been converted to Christianity by an English missionary sent from London by the same board that had first sent Father and Uncle Albert to China. He had earned his medical degree in Hongkong, and was an enlightened and forceful speaker against the Manchu dynasty of emperors who had been keeping China backward for so long. Most of the people were illiterate; they worked hard for almost nothing, and died by the thousands of flood, draught, disease, and famine. They considered boy babies more valuable than girl babies because boys could work, so female infanticide was

8

8 BEGINNINGS

common. This was especially true among the river people who were born, lived, and died on their boats clustered so thickly together that the bare masts looked like a burnt-out forest. Of the babies crawling along the decks, the boys had wooden blocks tied to their backs so that they would float if they fell overboard, but the girl babies had no such protection. We could not go outside our compound without having beggars tug at our sleeves. Many of them were disfigured, some of the children purposely by their parents so that by looking miserable they could become more efficient beggars. Meanwhile foreign imperalist nations, including the United States, were bleeding China dry.

In the excitement of cannon firing over our heads and Wuchang apparently on fire, we sat down for afternoon tea, my birthday party. We heard a commotion outside, and our whole compound was filled with soldiers carrying rifles. They wore white armbands, the insignia of the revolutionists. An undisciplined crowd, they laughed and milled about, some shooting their rifles into the air. A messenger came running up to our front door and handed Father a telegram. It was from the British Consul in Hankow (we were all British subjects then) giving us forty minutes to get out. Mother packed a few suitcases, put us in coats and hats, and bundled up Leslie, the last born, who was just six months old. We went out the front door and stood for a minute at the top of the high steps. Father said a short prayer. Then we walked slowly the hundred yards or so to the front gate of the compound. The rough-looking soldiers stopped jeering and parted to let us through.

We kept on walking (there were no rickshas in sight) to the *bund* on the Han River. Everywhere men were cutting off their pigtails and with shouts of joy tossing them up so that they hung from electric wires and balconies. Part of Sun Yat-sen's aim was to rid China of self-imposed signs of thralldom, among them the pigtail for men (long, carefully plaited, sometimes dirty, and always useless) and the bound feet for women.

At the river's edge Father hired a large sampan, paying a lot extra because the man said it was dangerous, he might get shot. In Hankow we went immediately to the British Consulate, where our family was assigned to the China Inland Mission to await steamer passage to Shanghai. After a week or so we boarded the *Tuck Wo*, owned by the Jardine-Mattheson Company, and set off on the three-day journey down the Yangtze to the safety of the international concessions in Shanghai.

Having offered his services to the Red Cross, Father returned to Hankow. There at the Presbyterian Hospital, with one other doctor, he operated practically day and night, often under shellfire, on the wounded soldiers of both sides.

By December the revolution had been "won" and a provisional "democratic" government set up with Yuen Shi-kai as president. Father returned to our empty home in Hanyang to pack up for our furlough, and when he entered the dining room (the servants of course had fled), there on the table were the tea things as we had left them, the jar of strawberry jam covered with mold. I have not seen the house where I was born since the revolution so hurriedly interrupted my ninth birthday "high tea." But the Chinese celebrate this day by setting off millions of firecrackers for the "double tenth," as they call it, the tenth day of the tenth month.

We went to England to visit relatives on an extended furlough, and then to America. Meanwhile two things happened. My parents were transferred from Hanyang to Shanghai Baptist College, on the Whangpoo River between Shanghai and Woosung. Mission secretaries sitting in their New York offices had sold Father's hospital, our home, and the whole compound to the Roman Catholics. This was called strategy. Also, Shanghai American School had been established to accommodate the children of American missionaries, diplomats, and business people living in the area. Seven miles from our new home, this was the old S.A.S. near Hongkew Park, where in the afternoons we used to watch the bearded and turbaned Shanghai Sikh policemen take off their trousers and run around the track. Gladys and I became weekly boarders. How we looked forward to Friday afternoon when our *mafoo* (horse driver) waited for us with the carriage outside the school gate! Getting nearer and nearer home we would sing happy songs and with shouts of joy finally enter the main gate of the college campus. Then home, and soft-boiled eggs in eggcups, platefuls of hot scones with butter and jam, and homemade ice cream. We thought of our schoolmates eating their Friday supper of weak vegetable soup and sago pudding. But late Sunday afternoon would always come, and with it "toward school with heavy looks."

Father's study was lined with Chinese dictionaries, Bible commentaries, medical books, and copies of the *Lancet* and the *Medical Journal*. When he was away teaching, I used to sneak in there and look at the pictures in Gray's *Anatomy*. I never told Wilfred and Leslie about this because they were too young to understand. In one wing of our house was the college dispensary, where at certain hours students and faculty could come for Father's prescriptions. One day a college student friend of mine was in there so long that we missed our tennis date. That evening, looking very grave, my parents took me into the study, closed the door, and told me that my friend would have to come every day for a treatment. Visiting a bad house in Shanghai where there were some immoral women, he had contracted some sort of dreadful disease. I was impressed but did not quite understand what was going on.

It was customary in China when somebody died for the members of the family to put the body in a great wooden coffin made of planks sometimes six inches thick (for the fairly well-off), and lay the coffin on top of the ground. They then consulted a priest to name a lucky day for burial, and this consisted of piling a huge mound of earth over the coffin and setting on fire paper replicas of houses, horses, carts, money—to comfort the soul of the deceased. The countryside was dotted with these mounds of earth, some of them in the middle of a rice field so that the farmer had to guide his water buffalo around them when plowing. Often the lucky day would not come for fifty or sixty years, and we children saw many an unburied coffin rotted away with white bones inside and ferns growing up between them.

At the supper table one night Father said he wished he had a skull so that he could really teach his premedical boys about the human head instead of just showing them lantern slides. Gladys and I looked at each other, for that afternoon we had seen a lovely skull almost falling out of one end of a crumpled coffin not two hundred yards from the main gate of the college.

The following Saturday we two went for a walk while Amah was giving the small boys their bath. We took along a piece of an old sheet. Sure enough, there was the skull just as we had first seen it. We carefully took it out, wrapped it in the cloth, and brought it home. Father was in his study. We knocked and said, "Here, Father, you said you needed a skull and we found one for you." We thought he would be thankful but he was furious. "Where did you get that?" he asked. We told him. Then he told us that this was grave-robbing, a serious offense; that these coffin sites are sacred and nobody should touch them. He added that we must get rid of it somehow, and not let anybody know, especially the servants.

At dusk Father, Gladys, and I went for a walk down by the pond, Father with a mysterious round object wrapped in cloth under his arm. Crouching around the skull, we stuffed pebbles into it until it wouldn't rattle. Then we climbed into the boat that was always moored there, and Father rowed us out. Gladys sat in the prow, and I sat in the stern with the skull between my knees. Father stopped rowing. "Now," he said, "may he rest in peace in the name of the Father and the Son and the Holy Ghost drop it in carefully sonny." I leaned over and laid the heavy white skull on the surface of the dark water. It sank.

Father would often go on weekend trips to give public-health lectures, and sometimes took me along to run the magic lantern. It was my job to keep his slides in good order and never put them in upside down. One spring Mother and Father took Gladys and me with them on a two-week lecture trip to Kinhwa—our spring vacation. We traveled entirely by boat on rivers and canals, except for a short twenty miles or so overland on a Chinese wheelbarrow. We loved sleeping on our houseboat, listening to the slapping of the water, the soft chatter of the three-man crew, and the creaking wooden sides. When we came to the rapids, Father bargained with twenty or thirty coolies to hitch themselves to long ropes and haul our houseboat over the rocks and through the dashing spray. This part of the river is called "Chi Li Lung" which means "the seven-mile dragon," and it looked like a dragon if you have ever seen one in New York or San Francisco.

We came to a great wide space, and the crew made a peculiar noise, half whistling and half humming, for more wind. We exchanged greetings with the cormorant fishermen as we drifted slowly by. All around us the hills, ablaze with tiger lilies, rose straight out of the water. "This is the end," I shouted, "we've got to turn back." And Father said, "That's not a terminus, sonny, only a bend in the river."

1   The Whole Comic Plot
of Falstaff

There have been more allusions to Falstaff than to any other Shakespearean character except Hamlet, and within the Falstaffian tetralogy *The Merry Wives of Windsor* has raised almost as many critical storms as *Hamlet* has. Both plays combine external problems with intriguing complexity of character, the one tragic and the other comic. Certainly, for *Merry Wives* the internal consistency of Falstaff and the chronology of the four plays in which he appears have graveled critics the most. The two problems are really one: the relationship of *Merry Wives* to the Hal-Falstaff quartet.

Scholars used to assign *Merry Wives* to the years between 1599 and 1602, but the researches of Leslie Hotson and more recently of William Green show that almost without a doubt the play was composed and performed for the investiture, on 21 April 1597 at Windsor Castle, of five new knights of the Garter, among them Lord Hunsden, chamberlain to Queen Elizabeth and patron of Shakespeare's theatrical company. Yet it is still customary for editors of the complete Shakespeare to give us the Falstaff plays in

---

The reader is probably aware of the famous names in the scholarly history of Falstaff: Bradley, Morgann, J. Dover Wilson, E. E. Stoll, Leslie Hotson, and others. Particularly recommended is a more recent work on the Garter background and dating of *The Merry Wives of Windsor* by William Green (Princeton, 1962). John Huntley and I worked on this problem together many years ago and never published the results; it was his initial idea, and to him belongs the victory, if any, in "persuasion."

the order of the first and second parts of *Henry IV*, then *Henry V*, and finally *The Merry Wives of Windsor*.

As for the character of Falstaff, some follow J. Dover Wilson's opinion that there are two Falstaffs: the Eastcheap original, and the Windsor cousin, a lascivious fool who sits ill with playgoers, readers, and critics. In fact, the handy *Oxford Companion to English Literature* puts the case nicely: "The Falstaff of Shakespeare's 'Merry Wives of Windsor' (q.v.), written to command, presents a very different character. A mere designing knave, with but few sparks of his former ingratiating humour, he cuts a sorry figure in the indignities and mortifications to which his vices expose him." Several theories attempt to justify this duality. Although Falstaff dies in *Henry V*, Elizabeth's specific (and possibly apochryphal) request to see Falstaff "in love" forced Shakespeare, some say, to resurrect him from the dead; the poet had to make the best of a bad thing and so failed. Another opinion suggests that although Shakespeare was willing to show Falstaff "in love," he had lost the knack of characterizing old Jack, as so often happens when an author attempts a sequel for a once-successful character. Still another view holds that Falstaff was originally the Oldcastle of *Famous Victories* and not entirely Shakespeare's. For these reasons and others, in most editions of selected plays of Shakespeare for classroom use, *The Merry Wives of Windsor* is omitted.

Assuming that Shakespeare was a master of his craft, I will essay an argument that when the plays are read with *Merry Wives* coming between *2 Henry IV* and *Henry V*, the character of Falstaff becomes a whole, cogent comic plot, with a beginning, middle, and end. Such literary analysis of *Merry Wives* corroborates recent textual and historical knowledge, and it uses the early eighteenth-century tradition about Queen Elizabeth in its favor rather than as an excuse for Shakespeare's nodding. Further, it brings to bear upon the problem the observed laws of social psychology and the analogy in dynamics of character-plotting between comedy and tragedy. Let us look at Falstaff's plot, then, in the order of *1 Henry IV*, *2 Henry IV*, *The Merry Wives of Windsor*, and *Henry V*.

In the first four acts of *1 Henry IV* a glorious Falstaff and his band of merry madcaps move in a world apart from the heroics and history of the rest of the play. In Falstaff are collected all the values and virtues of life at the Boar's Head: a wry wit, an instinct for roguery, and a love of good fellowship. He knows his limitations and the boundaries of his world, and is skeptical of the values of the other world, its honor, prestige, heroism, and responsibility. By repeatedly announcing his intention to reform and humorously blaming Hal for dragging him down, he reconciles the two. His love for the prince, he says (1. 2. 101–10), has bewitched his better judgment. When this jovial good humor is added to his age and girth, his love for sack, capon, and mild bawdry, Falstaff has more than earned the moral indulgence of his audience.

The planning of the Gadshill robbery, its execution, and the aftermath are all part of an elaborate game. Even if Falstaff cannot help being a rogue and a coward, he goes through the whole performance for the relish Hal gets out of it. "Stand and yield" is more of a sporting event than a crime. Back at the tavern, he acts as Poins and Hal had expected him to act, and the whole episode is jest enough for a week or even a month. Enjoying the immunity of love, Falstaff proceeds with the fantastic tale of the eleven men in buckram. When Hal checks him on the "three misbegotten knaves in Kendal green," Falstaff easily wriggles free, first refusing to speak on compulsion, then admitting and praising his instinctive love for the prince. The joke is done and both sides have played according to the rules they have invented: "Ah, no more o' that, Hal, an' thou lovest me" (2. 4. 312).

In his next scene Falstaff moves slightly out of bounds. Not yet in actions, nor in his intentions and general cast of mind, but in words alone Shakespeare prepares for his fall and Hal's rise. Falstaff abuses the hostess (3. 3. 61), and to bolster his position promises to cudgel the prince (101). When Hal enters to investigate this "eight-penny matter," Falstaff's wit again extricates him, and his apologies, though half-humorous, are sincere (184–96). From line 209 onward, Hal's change is abrupt (at least it is made to seem so to Falstaff, whereas we know from Hal's first soliloquy what to expect). The Prince curtly delegates responsibilities and exits with a ringing couplet:

> The land is burning: Percy stands on high;
> And either we or they must lower lie.
>
> [221–28]

Finally we see Falstaff the soldier and skeptic philosopher. War has become the business of the times, and Falstaff responds in his own way with his use of the "King's press," his catechism on honor (5. 2. 128–45), and his equivocation on the art of practical counterfeiting (5. 4. 111–31). But Hal is no longer playing the game. Falstaff's world has been invaded by other rules and other morals.

The fat knight overhears Henry's reaction to his and Hotspur's death, a speech that marks a midpoint in Hal's rise toward kingship (5. 4. 87–110), but he does not realize its implications. Though true to his principles in defining "the better part of valor," he fails to discern the boundaries of "discretion." After the epitaph on Hotspur (compared to Hal's remarks on Falstaff's "death"), there is something inherently morbid in Falstaff's rekilling Hotspur. We do not blame Hal for answering: "If a lie may do thee grace, I'll gild it with the happiest terms I have" (5. 4. 161–62). It is the promise of a friend. But suddenly everyone except Falstaff realizes that this is no longer the proper way to gain the grace of an heir apparent. The play ends.

In 2 *Henry IV*, Falstaff is raised in physical fortune, Hal furnishes him with a servant, money to buy a new coat, and a certain legal rather than a friendly immunity in return for his Shrewsbury service (1. 1). Although his evasions and retorts are almost as good-natured as before, he seems unaware that his present immunity comes to him by the rules of the world and not by the rules of his own game. An external change in situation, the removal of the prince, makes necessary a source of ready cash other than his royal friend's bounty, and this change must sooner or later bring about a change in his personality. A new means of livelihood, Mistress Quickly, presents itself, and she is ready to serve her warrant (2. 1). The street brawl brings the chief justice to remind Falstaff that without Hal's indulgence he must act by the rules of society; no longer may he "speak as having power to do wrong" (2. 1. 141).

Out of Hal's orbit, Falstaff turns from comradely drinking bouts to schemes of sexual adventure. Bardolph, whom he hired at Paul's "two and thirty years" ago, and the swaggering Pistol fill the gaps left in Falstaff's circle by the removal of Hal, Peto, and Poins. Falstaff's friends are progressively lowered in social and moral status, while Hal's are raised. Falstaff, in the company of professed rogues, not mere playboys, turns as a novice to the rules of a world whose counters are prestige, honor, and preferment. The scene at the Boar's Head (2. 2 and 4) is a conscious parallel with what he had once been. Before, he was only verbally out of bounds; now his very intentions are beyond the sanctions of common morality. In the first play Falstaff had described himself, and there is no evidence to contradict him: "That he is old, the more the pity, his white hairs do witness it; but that he is, saving your reverence, a whoremaster, that I utterly deny" (*I Hen. IV*,2. 4. 514). Now, however, with Quickly and Tearsheet, he is lowered in moral estate. In the first play, his "incomprehensible lies" were born of wit and knowledge; he allowed himself some bragging and was reprimanded for it by Hal. In the present play (2. 4) Falstaff both lies and boasts, but his wit is clouded by the trick being played upon him. He fails to mark the alacrity with which Hal ends the game, compared with Hal's leisure in the first play. He ignores the implications of Hal's words: "Give me my sword and cloak. Falstaff, good night." Rising again to the military situation, he no longer "lends the profession grace" but has become a professional thief in time of national peril.

Shallow is introduced, the lowest exemplar of what Falstaff is becoming. The battle scenes and the Colville incident pass. Shakespeare interposes the reconciliation of Hal and the chief justice (5. 2) before Pistol arrives in Gloucester to announce, "Sir John, thy tender lambkin now is King" (5. 3. 122). No other reaction but Falstaff's own would fit the developed lines of his character: "Choose what office thou wilt in the land, 'tis thine . . . my Lord Shallow . . . be what thou wilt; I am Fortune's steward . . . Come Pistol . . . devise something to do thyself good" (5. 3., 135–40). Falstaff has betrayed his relationship with Hal in the prospect of helping himself and his friends in advancement: "I know the young king is sick for me" (line 141). He is "riding for a fall" as surely as Macbeth.

If there is yet any doubt, Shakespeare shows Falstaff in London, vain and cocksure, boasting before friends and strangers. He imposes himself upon Hal publicly. Failing to recognize Hal's reaction as a rebuke, he hurries to meet him privately. His saving grace used to be the generation of wit and a good-humored knowledge of his position; now both have gone, and *hubris* has taken their place. Falstaff has brought upon himself Hal's "I know thee not, old man; fall to thy prayers." He is banished until the king hears that he has reformed (*2 Hen. IV*, 5. 5. 67–72).

In the traditional arrangement of the plays, unfortunately, *Henry*

V is read next. From the social and moral low point for Falstaff which we have just seen in the second part of *Henry IV, Henry V* contains an unexplained, seemingly arbitrary rise in Falstaff's character reflected in the dialogic narration of his death. In the hearts of his friends he becomes once more the beloved old Jack Falstaff. The solution to this problem may be found by considering *The Merry Wives of Windsor*, not *Henry V*, as that part of the Falstaff plot that comes next.

At the beginning of *Merry Wives*, Falstaff is the same Falstaff in character and estate we see at the end of *2 Henry IV*. In serious drama ignorance invariably leads to tragedy; in comedy, especially the corrective kind that Shakespeare is writing here and Jonson later perfected, ignorance dissipates itself in stupidity. As before, so here, Falstaff's wit, exercise it as he does with glory, is not sufficient to extricate him. His primary motivation is a lack of funds, which was consistently developed through *2 Henry IV*. Hal had promised him some subsistence, "that lack of means enforce you not to evils" (*2 Hen. IV*, 4. 5., 71), and is true to his word. Falstaff's secondary motivation is a lasciviousness instigated by Ford disguised as Brooke, again a motive carefully developed through the first two plays. Falstaff is now furthest removed from his original circle, the culmination of a series of events that strips him of every friendly exemption. Even Pistol and the newly introduced Nym (Anglo-Saxon *niman*, to take, to rob), "a yoke of his discarded men; very rogues now they be out of service," treacherously turn on Falstaff. Still bragging, Falstaff is stupidly blind to the fact that he is no longer controlling but is being controlled.

Hence the major action of *Merry Wives* must be Falstaff's cleansing, correction, and eventual rise in moral estate, for in the two parts of *Henry IV* he has so entwined himself in our hearts that we are not willing to lose him. In tragedy a discovery usually precedes a reversal, and if Falstaff is to be "saved" he must realize (in this comic plot) something fundamental about himself and the world as it really is. His purgation is psychologically and morally appropriate in *Merry Wives*, making the upward movement in Falstaff's character both necessary and probable.

A double situation precipitates the action: a split in ranks and Falstaff's need for money to appease his expanding appetites. He and his "discarded men" have provoked Shallow and his cousin Slender, and the characters enlist themselves in one or the other camp. Before the conflict goes very far, Ann Page enters, and a split ensues in Shallow's forces. A prize has been introduced far more delectable than the vindication of Shallow's honor. In act 1, scene 3, the same split riddles Falstaff's forces, and he has to leave Bardolph to mine Host of the Garter. The need for cash, however, is more important than maintaining a haughty demeanor before Shallow; and the solution—"I mean to make love to Ford's wife"— more enticing. Both Pistol and Nym, their "honor" impugned by the suggestion of playing Sir Pandarus, desert Falstaff to inform Page and Ford of this "French thrift."

Falstaff plunges into his adulterous scheme for wealth by sending duplicate letters. Duplicate letters are worthy of Falstaff at the end of *2 Henry IV*, whose pride has strangled his wit and whose knowledge is now to the rear of his action. Of course the love letters inform the world of his plans and immediately turn him into a helpless dupe of his own plot. Even before the first assault, the wives have compared notes, as could be well expected, and Ford is pushing the ignorant Falstaff closer and closer to the edge of destruction with flattery and money. And yet Falstaff airily brags to Ford himself that "I will use her as the key of the cuckoldly rogue's coffer; and there's my harvest home" (2. 2. 285).

At this point Shakespeare's artistry in social psychology is seen at its best. The "merry wives" now, in contrast to the "merry madcaps" whom Falstaff used to lead, are making the rules of the game. A reluctant follower, Falstaff is hoist with his own brand of petard. The buck basket and the ducking in Dachet lane signal the necessary punishment by these comic furies. In soliloquy Falstaff says: "Have I liv'd to be carried in a basket and to be thrown in the Thames like a barrow of butcher's offal? Well, if I be serv'd another trick, I'll have my brains ta'en out and butter'd, and give them to a dog for a new-year's gift" (3. 5. 5–8). But it takes three strokes of the lash, not just one, to raise Falstaff from his depravity to see himself for what he is.

After the ducking, the sagacious Mistress Page prescribes further treatment: "We will yet have more tricks with Falstaff. His dissolute disease will scarce obey this medicine" (3. 3. 204). Her diagnosis is accurate, for in the next scene Shakespeare shows Falstaff forgetting his half-humorous soliloquy and acting the blind braggart before Quickly and "Brooke." The second corrective episode parallels the first: the audience is given a full preview.

Falstaff enters and hides, Ford and the rest search for him, and Falstaff's chastisement in ignominious escape strikes deeper. The first corrective was mainly fear at being discovered in the basket, and the physical punishment was represented offstage. Now, as "the witch of Brainford," dressed in billowing female garb, Falstaff is pummeled on stage, and with due respect for his gift for hyperbole, the insult to his fat frame is not mild. Previously he confessed his sins to himself, but soon, in his descent from pride, he will admit his faults to the host: "Ay, that there was, mine host; one that hath taught me more wit than ever I learn'd before in my life; and I paid nothing for it neither, but was paid for my learning" (4. 5. 60–61). The buck basket and the Brainford episodes are both more or less private affairs. Falstaff himself hardly realizes that he is being played for the fool, and only the two wives and Quickly are in on the joke.

Mrs. Ford, Falstaff's original "prey," rightly perceives that a public application of the medicine will be a third and last: "I'll warrant they'll have him publicly sham'd; and methinks there would be no period to the jest, should he not be publicly sham'd" (4. 2. 234). So the whole Fairy episode is laid out (4. 4). The Queen Fairy's song (5. 5. 96–106) is a sermon for Falstaff. He is thereupon pinched, pulled, burned, and finally ridiculed by Page and Ford and their two merry Windsor wives. At the beginning of the play Falstaff considered these worthies only an apt audience for his boasts; now the situation is reversed. Falstaff's awakening from his dream is perhaps as effective on the comic stage as Othello's final discovery of himself as "the base Indian [who] threw a pearl away richer than all his tribe." Falstaff says, "I do begin to perceive that I am made an ass" (5. 5. 125). At last he has touched upon his moral disease, and immediately Shakespeare reflects those emotions he wants us to feel in the surrounding characters: "Yet be cheerful, knight. Thou shalt eat a posset tonight at my house" (line 180). The whole company exits, a happy, merry, friendly band, "Sir John and all."

Without this comic catharsis in *The Merry Wives of Windsor*, the treatment in *Henry V* would be inexplicable. The reflected good will at the end of *Merry Wives* attends Falstaff when he is made to die. The emotion felt for him is sadness at his departure, garnished with rough, good-humored love. The memory of Falstaff as he once was temporarily resolves the quarrel between Nym, Pistol, and Bardolph, and each in his turn gives an epitaph, "for Falstaff is dead, and we must ern therefore." Mistress Quickly's narration, "a' babbled o' green fields," and Bardolph's comment, "Would I were with him, wheresome-er he is, either in heaven or in hell" (2. 3), aptly express the loyalty that an old friend has rewon for himself.

Whatever moral evaluation Shakespeare intended, one ventures to say that he found it not in his heart to throw Falstaff off with the rest, but to restore him through the chastisement of *The Merry Wives of Windsor*. In my suggested sequence, the four Falstaff plays present us with a changing character consistent with the principles of comic plot. Falstaff's fortunes are plotted through an initial rise, a fall through excess, a chastening and discovery of self, and finally (in *Henry V*) a death that reconciles him with fellowship and "heaven."

Shakespeare had to finish the Falstaff story. Either he was commanded or an opportunity presented itself for his company to present a "Garter-play" at Windsor. Elizabeth either would or would not be there to see it, but the knights of the Garter would be in the audience, and most prominently Lord Hunsden. Fortuitously Shakespeare was given, within three weeks, a better way to end the Falstaff plot than he had planned at the end of *2 Henry IV*, a better way than taking him to France, probably there to hang him with Nym under the king's orders.

My suggested ordering of the plays credits the 1702 assertion of Dennis that Elizabeth liked *The Merry Wives* on grounds of decorum, for she was an unusually well educated and perceptive lady. Dennis wrote:

> That this Comedy was not despicable, I guess'd for several Reasons: First, I knew very well, that it has pleas'd one of the greatest Queens that ever was in the World, great . . . for her knowledge of Polite Learning, and her nice taste of the Drama, for such a taste we may be sure she had, by the relish which she had of the Ancients. This comedy was written at her Command, and . . . as Tradition tells us she was very well pleas'd at the Representation.

Seven years later, in 1709, Nicholas Rowe reported that the Queen "was so well pleas'd with that admirable Character of *Falstaff*, in the two Parts of *Henry* the Fourth, that she commanded him to continue it for one Play more, and to shew him in Love."

It is no part of that tradition that Shakespeare, having killed off Falstaff in *Henry V*, revived him in *The Merry Wives of Windsor*, and so failed. There are not two Falstaffs, only one.

2   Who Wrote the First Two Cambridge *Parnassus* Plays?

As part of their Christmas festivities in 1598, 1599, 1600, and 1601, the young men of Saint John's, Cambridge, presumably aided by any other collegians they could draft, produced the three so-called *Parnassus* plays. Because of their sheer fun, topical value, and literary merit, they have aroused a great deal of interest. The first play, *The Pilgrimage to Parnassus*, describes Studioso and Philomusus on their way to the B.A. degree. Passing through the "countries" of Logic, Rhetoric, and Philosophy, they resist with some difficulty three characters who would tempt them from the narrow path: a winebibber, a drooling Puritan, and a lover of erotic verse. In the next play, *The Returne from Parnassus*, the young men, having graduated, are set adrift in the real world. Discovering that nobody is willing either to buy their poetry or pay them a living wage as chaplain or schoolmaster, they threaten to accept the bribe for "perverting" to Rome. The final play is entitled *The Returne from Parnassus; or, The Scourge of Simony*. The similarity of titles has led some to think of the last two plays together, but the manuscript evidence shows that the final play was once called "The Progresse," meaning "the progress in their misery." It opens with the boys reading Bodenham's newly published *Belvedere; or, The Muses' Garden* (1600) and lampooning practically every contemporary poet in it. Each play increases in the acerbity of its satire, the final play containing fierce attacks on

---

I am convinced that Joseph Hall wrote the last play in the Parnassan trilogy. The full argument here for the authorship of the first two plays has not heretofore been published.

Marston and on current social conditions. Twice acted (1600, 1601) and twice printed (1606), it stood alone until W. D. Macray, the Bodleian's librarian, discovered in Thomas Hearne's manuscript collection the earlier two plays and published the first edition of the comic trilogy (1886).[1]

Referring to the plays as "The Pilgrimage," "The Returne," and "The Progresse," I shall attempt to persuade my readers that the first pair of plays was written by John Weever of Queen's. That a poet from another college should be invited to take part in a dramatic project of John's, especially during Christmas vacation, is not surprising. In 1597, the festivities that welcomed the earl of Essex to Cambridge were undertaken by Sutton of King's, Stanton of John's, Sharton of Trinity, and Braithwaite and Hall from Emmanuel.[2] My brief for John Weever rests on three overlapping propositions: (1) that consideration of the first two plays as a single dichotomous unit may revise our speculations on the dates of performance; (2) that the prologue to the second play, despite our paucity of biographical information, points to John Weever; and (3) parallels exist between Weever's known works and the first two *Parnassus* plays.

Any discussion of authorship must begin with the verse prologue of the third play:

> In Scholers furtunes twise forlorne and dead
> Twise hath our weary pen earst laboured,
> Making them Pilgrims to *Pernassus* hill,
> Then penning their returne with ruder quill.
> Now we present vnto each pittying eye
> The schollers progresse in their miserye.
>
> [Lines 70–75]

From this Leishman accepts G. C. Moore's suggestion that the first play was not written by the author of the second; and that the second and third plays were written by the same man. The reasoning rests on a "rule" of prologue writing, that you exalt your predecessor while disparaging yourself, coupled with the meaning of "ruder quill."

Rather than making the break between number one and number two and three, however, I interpret the last two lines after the full stop to intend a separation of number three from numbers one and two, with the words "now" and "progresse." The addition of the subtitle to the printed version of the final play, "Or the Scourge of Simony," emphasizes this.

The "ruder quill," moreover, does not necessarily mean a different author in an apologetic frame of reference. The word "rude" may describe the satirical style based on the notion that "satire" is related to "satyr," hence "goat," and a rough, shaggy kind of writing in which obscurity is a virtue. So in 1597 Hall opened his first volume of satires with:

> That Euny should accost my Muse and mee,
> For this so *rude* and recklesse Poesie.[3]

As the personal invective increases, the censorius style becomes "ruder" or more "crabbed" (as Persius was called "crabbed") and more difficult to pin down as a means of escaping libel. Thus "ruder quill" may introduce not a different author but merely a different style.

Several other arguments may be made for putting the first two plays together and assuming for them a single author. Manuscript and linguistic evidence links them; together they appear in twenty folio pages in the same hand, upon the outside leaf of which is the name of a one-time owner, "Edmunde Rishton, Lancastrensis." The manuscript contains northern forms of language that do not appear in the final play.[4] The length of the plays, moreover, would indicate that the first two may have gone together as a single performance in two parts, or "shows," as they were called. "The Pilgrimage" is only 720 lines long, less than one-third of the final play. The first pair of plays combined amount to 2,291 lines, making them just about even with the last play, which is 2,223 lines long.[5] Finally, a key passage near the beginning of the third play, besides asserting that the *Parnassus* plays had performances during four successive Christmas seasons, implies that the first two plays went together and had more than one performance:

> *Momus.* Humours indeed: is it not a pretty humor to stand hammering vpon two *indiuiduum vagum.* 2. schollers, some foure yeare? . . . The Pilgrimage to *Pernassus,* and the returne from *Pernassus,* haue stood the honest *Stagekeepers,* in many a Crownes expence for linckes and vizards: purchas'd [many] a Sophister a knock with a clubbe, hindred the buttlers box, and emptied the Colledge Barrrells; and now, vnlesse you haue heard the former, you may returne home [againe] as wise as you came. [Lines 33–44]

The custom of referring, with no manuscript or printed evidence, to the last two plays as "The *First*" and "The *Second* Returne" has tended to make us think of the last two plays as a pair. If, on the other hand, the first two are linked, then we may speculate further on the dates of performance. Leishman furnishes no proof apart from the probable time of composition based on allusions to contemporary publications. The initial pair of plays might well have had their first performance at Christmas 1598. Then if a second performance of the pair were given at Christmas 1599, with a few allusions to bring it up to date, a new prologue, which we are about to examine, could have been fitted to the second play to explain that something drastic had happened between the two performances. Because of his peculiar gifts in wielding a "ruder quill" such action may have been taken against John Weever as the author of the first two *Parnassus* plays.

The prologue to "The Returne" is a fine example of the "rude" satirical style—rough and enigmatic. This kind of style begot Marston's double "reactio" to Hall's *Vergidemiae* of anger for imagined vilification and admiration for Hall's stylistic involution:

> Helpe to vnmaske the Satyres secresie,
> Delphick Apollo, ayde me to vnrip
> These darke Enigmaes, and strange ridling sense.[6]

In a game of charades the author's name is hidden but is meant to be guessed. After the speaker of the prologue has uttered the single word "Gentle...," as if to say, "Gentle spectators, in our last play...," the Stagekeeper interrupts him with

How, *gentle* saye youe, cringinge parasite?	1
That scrapinge legg, that doppinge courtisie,	2
That fawninge bowe, those sycophants smoothe tearmes	3
Gained our stage muche fauoure, did they not?	4
Surelie it made our poet a staide man,	5
Kepte his proude necke from baser lambskins weare,	6
Had like to haue made him senior sophister.	7
He was faine to take his course by Germanie	8
Ere he coulde gett a silie poore degree.	9
Hee neuer since durst name a peece of cheese,	10
Though Chessire seems to priuiledge his name.	11

> His looke was neuer sanguine since that daye,   12
> Nere since he laughte to see a mimick playe.   13
> Sirra be gone, you play noe prologue here . . .   14

By omitting the first four lines and interpreting all that follows
as pertaining only to "The Pilgrimage," Leishman misses the abrupt change in tone, beginning with the fifth line, and the possible
irony. The prologue to the previous play begins, "Spectators, take
youe noe seuere accounte / Of our two pilgrims to Parnassus
mount." The interruption signals that the prologue to the second
play was, at its first performance, as "gentle" as the prologue to
the first play. Did these smooth sycophantic terms "gain our stage
much favor?" They may have at first, but, look what has happened
since to our author. We'll have no "gentle" prologue now.

Because of his contribution to "our stage" the author was (temporarily) "stayed" in his college course. He stood up to authority so
defiantly (proud necke," line 6) that he risked failing the B. A.
degree. But he was only "likely" to have become "senior sophis-
ter" (line 7). As a matter of fact, John Weever, admitted to Queen's
on 10 April 1594, received his degree in 1597/8, the usual time.[7]

Could the threat of "staying" the author have been made to John
Weever? Writing any kind of satire had suddenly become dangerous, and Weever was already known for his *Epigrammes* (1599). If
there were two performances of the double *Parnassus* play, then
something drastic did happen between the two performances: the
order of 1 June 1599 from Archbishop Whitgift and the bishop of
London to have certain books "called in" and proscribed for their
lewdness, personal invective, and dangerous criticism of the
establishment. The list included books by Joseph Hall, John
Marston, Guilpin, Davies, Marlowe, Middleton, all the controversy between Nashe and Harvey, and Cutwode's *Caltha
Poetarum*. Three days later many of the books were publicly
burned at Stationers' Hall, but Hall's and Cutwode's were "staid,"
that is, reprieved.[8] Valentine Simmes, who printed Weever's *Epigrammes*, was one of those individually warned by the Stationers'
Company.[9] If word got out that Weever had written these plays
containing allusions to two proscribed writers, Marston and
Nashe, the authorities, anxious for the university's reputation,
might well have threatened to send him down.

Lines 8 and 9 of the Prologue tell us that the author "was fain"
to travel by way of Germany before he could get his degree.

But surely, in this kind of purposefully enigmatic writing, the lines are not to be taken literally. The phrase "by Germanie" may allude to the author's drinking habits, thus implying that he was delayed for reasons of personal behavior as well. The stereotype of the drunken German was repeated by practically every English traveler to that country. Corryatt in his *Crudities,* for example, says, "Truly I have heard Germany much despised for drunk-ennesse before I saw it." He describes the Germans' drinking "helter-skelter": "It is their custome whensoever they drink to another to see their glasses filled up incontinent ... and thus they deliver it into the hand of him to whome they drinke, esteeming him a very curteous man that doth pledge the whole, according to the old verse, *Germanus mihi frater eris si pocula siccas.*"[10] Another traveler, Fynes Moryson, notes the huge casks of wine in Germany and the enthusiasm with which they were drained: "To their drinking they can prescribe no meane nor end.... And to say truth, the Germans are in high excesse subject to this vice of drinking."[11] There follow several eyewitness accounts of alcoholic excess by Germans, ranging from vomiting in their dinner com-panions' laps and pissing under the table to murder during a drunken frenzy. We know little of Weever's life, but he may have failed to resist one of the three tempters of "The Pilgrimage to Parnassus," Madido the drunkard, who almost persuades the two pilgrims to stop at every tavern along the way; and there was a great deal of drinking at these college dramatic performances.[12]

What are "cheese" and "Cheshire" doing here (lines 10–11)? Weever was a Lancastrian, and there is no more evidence of his distaste for cheese than there is for his addiction to malt. Cheese and Cheshire make an inevitable pair, but the clearest hint is that the principal river in Cheshire is the River Weaver. If the author is John Weever and the main river in Cheshire is the Weaver, then, of course, "Cheshire seems to privilege his name" (line 11). John Weever knew this. Inspired by the furor over Shakespeare's init-ially naming Falstaff Sir John Oldcastle and determined to rescue the gentleman's status as martyr, Weever published in 1601 *The Life and Death of Sir John Oldcastle, Knight.* Oldcastle speaks the poem, and at one juncture Weever brings him to Cheshire and the banks of the river whose name the author proudly shares:

> Through many bywaies, many countries fle[d],
> In midst of Cheshire now I am on a river,

> By more crookt winding which curr[ent led],
> Then I had done by wayes: her name the W[eev]er;
> On whose prowde banke such entertaine I had,
> As longer, if I might, I would have staid.[13]

We shall have more to say about Weever, Sir John Oldcastle, and Falstaff.

A curious piece of evidence form Weever's long preamble "To the Vayne-Glorious" in his *Whipping of the Satyre* (1601) links "Cheshire" and "cheese" and the satirical effect of epigram. To the "Epigrammatist" (Guilpin) Weever scoffs: "You make more reckoning of a Iest, then a scholler doth of a Maundy Thursday, or Cheshireman of the New-found well." A Guilpin epigram, Weever continues, "doth nothing but make way for the last two lines, which are brought in like a piece of cheese and a manchet [small piece of bread], to digest all that went before."[14] Could Weever have jocularly used this simile in conversation about the art of epigrammatic satire, but now, after the official injunction, dare not "name a piece of cheese"?

Lines 12–13 of this Prologue to "The Returne" continue the thought that ever since he saw "a mimic play" the author has become a rather serious person. This would bring to mind that the word "staid" in line 5 may mean not only "kept back" but also no longer the *bon vivant* of yore. He has become "staid," that is, "of grave or sedate deportment; dignified and serious in demeanor or conduct" (OED). The greater the exaggeration of reform, the funnier the description would be to the audience that heard it.

From this very prologue several attempts have been made to identify the author, none of them very convincing because the evidence is unrealistic and because they are all directed toward "The Pilgrimage" rather than "The Pilgrimage" and "The Returne." For example, it has been argued that William Dodd of Cheshire, a student at John's, wrote the first play. Again John Day, who sometimes spelled his name "Dey," which means dairy or a maker of cheese, has been thought to be the author. It has even been proposed that by "Germanie" is meant Holland, hence William Holland wrote the first play.[15] The lines say that we will not have a "gentle prologue," which may have brought forth applause before. The reason for stopping the speaker's "sycophantic terms" is that (in semijocular phrases) the author has since been reprimanded. His name is better concealed in a series of "guess who" jokes, which were understood by the audience of undergraduates united solidly behind one of their own against master and beadle. These archly veiled hints, apparently written for a second performance of the pair of plays at Christmas, 1600/1601, point more directly to John Weever than to any other candidate so far named.

The absence of details of Weever's life habits and personality can be partially compensated for by a reading of his known publications, which contain many parallels to the first two Parnassus plays. *Epigrammes in the Oldest Cut and Newest Fashion* (1599), published the year after Hall's second volume, when Weever was twenty-three years old, admits him to the circle of young satirists who burst upon the literary scene during the final years of Elizabeth's reign. His *Epigrammes* link him to the Marston-Hall quarrel, two satirists very much involved in the *Parnassus* trilogy and the official censuring of 1599. Weever admires Marston and dismisses Hall. In his next publication, *Faunus and Melliflora* (1600), however, he makes a *volte face*, attacking Marston and praising Hall. Davenport writes, "Something must have caused a change in Weever's feelings."[16] I believe that the "something" was his part in the *Parnassus* plays, coupled with the fact that in the censuring of 1599 Marston's works were officially condemned and Hall's just as officially reprieved.

Of more significance to my thesis is that the character Gullio in "The Returne" refers to Weever's epigram on Gullio:

> [Second Week] *Epig. 21 In obitum sepulcrum Gullionis.*
> Here lies fat *Gullio*, who caperd in a cord
> To highest heau'en for all his huge great weight,
> His friends left at *Tiburne* in the yere of our Lord
>   1   5   9   and   8
> What part of his body French men did not eate,
> That part he giues freely to worms for their meat.[17]

Unless one could say that the poor wretch has been "gulled" into being hanged, this "fat Gullio" seems etymologically related to "gule," "gullet"—to swallow, to gorge; he seems to have been a "glutton."

As the prologue to "The Returne" contains a xenophobic

stereotype of the German people, this epigram makes fun of the Frenchman's gustatory pursuits. The cuisine of *le fol Français* demanded the custom of *hanging* venison or game until it was practically rotten. Fynes Moryson observed that "the French alone delight in mortified meates."[18] Under "mortified" the OED cites a passage from Robert Ashley's 1594 translation of *Loys le Roy* on "mortifying raw flesh," and Massinger's "worthy loyne of Veale... Mortified to grow tender" (*Maid of Honour*, 3. 1). Weever's *fat hanged* Englishman, then, might furnish forth a "mortified" feast for Frenchmen—witty, perhaps, but not very funny.

The fact that no one has been able to identify a criminal who was legally (one would suppose) hanged at Tyburn in 1598 should give us pause. We have already noted Weever's interest in restoring the reputation of Sir John Oldcastle, and later we shall see how well acquainted Weever was with Shakespeare's *Henry IV* plays. Is it possible that from a production of both parts of Henry IV in London Weever received his inspiration for the epigram and for his defense of Oldcastle as martyr? The old *Famous Victories of Henry the Fifth*, in which the original of Falstaff appears as Sir John Oldcastle, was printed in 1598. Both parts of Shakespeare's *Henry IV* were written by 1598, and even after Lord Cobham requested Shakespeare to change the name of his fat braggart, Shakespeare had difficulty remembering to do so (*1 Hen. IV*, 1. 1., 47). The fat Gullio hanged in 1598 saying goodbye to his friends sends us back to Falstaff, Bardolph, Nym, Shallow, and the rest; and to Shakespeare's apology. In part 1 (5. 4, 107) when Oldcastle-Falstaff falls on the ground pretending he had slain Hotspur, Hal says: "Death hath not struck so fat a deer today." In the final scene of that play, the speech of Hal as king beginning, "I know thee not, old man; fall to thy prayers" (lines 51 ff.) turns the corpulent knight into one of the greatest "gulls" of all time, and asks him to "mortify the flesh" in prayer. The conversation that follows between Oldcastle-Falstaff and Shallow may play a part in Weever's epigram with its reference to eating and hanging:

> FAL. Sir, I will be as good as my word. This that you heard
> was but a colour [pretext].
> SHAL. A colour [collar, hangman's noose] that I fear you
> will die in, Sir John.

FAL. Fear no colours [choler?]?; go with me to dinner . . . .
CHIEF JUSTICE. Go, carry Sir John Falstaff to the Fleet.

And what about Weever's epigrammatic allusion to French-men's meat? Shakespeare's apology for first naming the fat Falstaff Sir John Oldcastle comes in the epilogue of part 2:

> One word more, I beseech you. If you be not too much cloy'd with *fat meat,* our humble author will continue the story, with Sir John in it, and make you merry with *fair Katharine of France;* where, for anything I know, *Falstaff shall die of a sweat,* unless already 'a be killed with your hard opinions; for Oldcastle died a martyr, and this is not the man. [My italics]

In effect, the year 1598 witnessed an execution for libel visited upon the fat-braggart-who-went-by-the-name-of-Sir-John-Old-castle, and John Weever is glad of it.

The character Gullio in *Parnassus* who quotes Weever's epigram on Gullio, is a foolish courtier, a self-styled lover-swordsman, and an ignorant patron of poets. Imagine the burst of laughter that must have greeted his reference (placed there, I believed, by Weever) to Weever's epigram that obviously the pretender to learning had never read:

> I am verie latelie registered in the roules of fame, in an Epigram made by a Cambridge man, one Weauer—fellow, I warrant him, els coulde he neuer haue had such a quick sight into my vertues, howsoeuer I merit his praise: if I meet with him I will vouchsafe to giue him condigne thankes. ["The Returne," lines 957ff.]

Other epigrames by Weever show an intense interest in the theater that may well have brought him into the *Parnassus* plays at St. John's. Epigram no. 6 of the Second Week refers to the spec-tators of Kyd's *Spanish Tragedy.* Epigram 23, Fourth Week, is ad-dressed to Edward Alleyn, partner of Henslowe, half-owner of the Fortune Theatre, and chief actor in the Lord Admiral's Company. And Weever's address to Shakespeare (Epigram 22, Fourth week), the only attempt at a sonnet among the *Epigrammes,* stands as one of the earliest recognitions of our greatest dramatic poet and shares the fondness for Shakespeare's erotic poems with Amoretto, the lovesick litterateur of *Parnassus.* Gullio in "The Re-

turne" will put "sweet Mr. Shakespeare's *Venus and Adonis* vnder
my pillow" (lines 1203–4), but in "The Progresse" Judicio's sterner
voice wishes that Shakespeare could have been content "without
loues foolish languishment" (ines 301–4). After the public burning
of Nashe's *Choice of Valentines* and Guilpin's *Skialetheia*, it became
the fashion to condemn erotic verse.

A few months after the *Epigrammes*, Weever published a curious
piece, *Faunus and Melliflora* (1600). It starts out as an amorous
poem filled with allusions to "Hero and Leander" and "Venus and
Adonis." After a thousand lines or so of gaudy eroticism,
Weever's *Faunus and Melliflora* suddenly turns into a mythological
"history" of satire, and finally, with some crudely interspersed
translations from Horace and Persius, into a condemnation of all
satire. Although, as we saw, in the *Epigrammes* Weever placed
Marston ahead of Hall, here he disapproves of Marston's *Scourge
of Villanie* and quotes with approval Hall's *Vergidemiae*. The clue to
this strange mixture of genres and reversed personal allegiance is,
once more, the archbishop's condemnation, on 1 June 1599, of
certain satires to the bonfire, which Weever recounts at the end of
his "history." Venus, angry at all satirists, craves a boon:

> That all the Satyres then in England liuing
> Should sacrifisde be in the burning fire,
> To pacifie so great a goddesse ire,
> And from their Cyndars should a Satyre rise,
> Which their Satyricke snarling should despise.
> All which perform'd, she left our English shore,
> Neuer I hope to trouble vs any more.
>
> [Lines 1573–79]

The year after *Faunus and Melliflora*, Weever really joined the
ranks of the antisatirists in *The Whipping of the Satyre* (1601). It is
addressed to the "Satyrist, Epigrammatist, and Humourist," who
are very probably Marston, Guilpin, and Ben Jonson. The subtitle
of this pamphlet, "The Pilgrims Story" recalls the two "pilgrims"
who make their joyful "Pilgrimage to Parnassus" and their sober
"Returne." The following lines from *The Whipping*—"I' le haue the
maner of the combate all, / Painted in colours by some Picturer, /
And haue it vp vpon my studie wall" (248–50)—seem to echo
Gullio's speech in "The Returne"—"O sweet Mr. Shakespeare, Ile
haue his picture in my studie at the court" (line 1032). A clear

allusion to Shakespeare's *Henry IV* comes in *The Whipping;* it is addressed to Marston, that "masty dog" (line 156):

> I dare here speake it, and my speech mayntayne,
> That Sir Iohn Falstaffe was not any way
> More grosse in body, then you are in brayne.
>
> [Lines 433–37]

Weever's apparent reformation is made complete in his final poem, which we have already glanced at for its vindication of Sir John Oldcastle as a true martyr to the Lollard cause rather than the fat drinking braggart depicted in Falstaff. A connection between this literary effort and the *Parnassus* plays may lie in the number of echoes they contain of Shakespeare's *1* and *2 Henry IV*. Ingenioso in "The Pilgrimage" speaks of Host John of the Crown as crying "Anon anon Sir" (line 626). The drunken Madido cries out: "Zouns, I want a worde miserably . . . I shall noe sooner open this pint pot, but the words like a knave tapster will crie anon anon sr. (He drinks)" ("The Pilgrimage," lines, 163–65). The same character later mentions the "Halfe Moon" as one of the rooms in the tavern, and in *1 Henry IV* we have "Anon anon sir, Score a Pint of Bastard in the Halfe Moone" (2. 4., 29).

The June 1599, injunction against lewd poetry and personal invective that condemned to the fire the works of Marston and Nashe among others must be the reason not only for Weever's changing directions in his own poetry but also for keeping hidden his part, if any, in the early satirical *Parnassus* plays at Cambridge. The guessing-game characterization of the author of the first two plays in the prologue to the second play can be made to fit Weever without great exaggeration. And Weever's acknowledged works shows a fondness for the stage and a familiarity with Shakespeare's poems and plays that were written before 1599, a familiarity shared by the speakers in the first pair of *Parnassus* plays.

In three hundred and eighty years not a single piece of direct evidence has come to light. All we can do is to throw a circumstantial net around John Weever as probably their author.

3   Why Ben Jonson
Did Not Claim
The Case Is Altered

Whether or not Jonson wrote *The Case Is Altered* is still an open question.[1] Though it was probably acted before 1598, it was not printed until 1609. Of the quarto copies thus produced, some have "Beniamen Ionson" printed in capital letters at the top of the title page; others have no author's name; and still others have "Written by Ben. Ionson," the type crowded into the center of the title page.[2] Neither Jonson nor any contemporary attest the play to be by Jonson; and Jonson did not include it in the 1616 folio of his collected plays. Apart from the dubious 1609 title-page attribution of a 1597 play, history is silent as to who wrote it.

It was not until 1756 that *The Case Is Altered* was assigned to Ben Jonson, by Peter Whalley, on the evidence of the quartos just described.[3] The play struck the eighteenth-century Mr. Whalley as the kind of good "Shakespearean" comedy that he wished Jonson had written more of: "It is greatly to be wished indeed, that Jonson had possessed that poetic passion, and power to touch the heart, which would have made his dramas universal; and equally felt and understood in all ages."[4] *The Case Is Altered* combines two Plautine plots in a semihistorical setting; to the story of miserly Jacques and his "daughter" is added some tender love interest; and there are two marvelous fools, Onion and Juniper. Since 1756, every Jonson scholar has tried hard to think of it as a Jonsonian

---

This essay appeared in different form as "Ben Jonson and Anthony Munday; or, *The Case Is Altered* Altered Again," in *Studies in English Drama Presented to Baldwin Maxwell, Philological Quarterly* 41 (1962): 205–14.

play. The two most elaborate arguments are those of Selin (1917) and of Enck (1957).

Selin[5] admits there is no historical proof that Jonson wrote it; so he relies on his five kinds of internal proof. First, of the dozens of parallel passages to Jonson's other plays, few are convincing. There is only one really parallel passage: between *The Case Is Altered*, 2. 7., 76–82 (Valentine's speech about the theaters in Utopia[6]) and a speech by Asper at the beginning of *Every Man Out*.[7] We shall discuss this later. Secondly, Selin confesses his vocabulary test is inconclusive: the word "humour" is used fourteen times in *The Case Is Altered* but twenty-six times in Shakespeare's *Merry Wives*. Third, as for characters, the merry talk of Juniper and Onion "sounds like" that of Cob and Orange in *Every Man Out*; and Jacques's suspicious nature is "like" that of Kitely and of Volpone. Fourth, "situations" that characterize a prevailing humour, such as travel, fencing, tobacco, courtship, etc., are also seen in Jonson's plays (not to mention plays by other authors). Finally, in prosody, Selin's counting shows that feminine endings exist in the same ratio that polysyllabic words do, an incomprehensible statistic.

Enck's argument for Jonson is stronger.[8] He finds external aid in the fact that Jonson copied out in longhand for his *Chorus Poetarum* passages of Plautus's *Aulularia*, one of the very comedies "he had appropriated for *The Case Is Altered*." Enck's main argument is that an analysis not of minor parallel parts but of whole assumptions in character portrayal and plot formation shows that *The Case Is Altered* is an archetypal humors comedy in which several sets of characters discover their true identity. The cogency of this analysis, however, raises one problem while settling another. If *The Case Is Altered* is so good, why did not Jonson claim it as an example of his peculiar contribution to English classical comedy? The fact is that even omitting the Balladino incident, the play shows evidence of having been patched together.

My hypothesis is that Jonson took an old play written by his enemies in the *poetamachia* and refurbished its beginning to strike back at them, particularly Anthony Munday; and that Munday, therefore, had the greatest hand in the original composition.

My case rests on two propositions generally agreed upon: (1) that the original play was popular before 1600, and (2) that the sketch of Antonio Balladino is Jonson's satire on Munday interpolated after 1600 by grafting the silly poet onto the character Valentine. The two propositions are really one and so much a part of the history of the play that Enck could accomplish his brilliant exegesis only by omitting it.[9]

The play was well known before 1600. In *Palladis Tamia* (1598), Meres had accorded Jonson a place in tragedy but, after speaking of the Greeks in comedy, said: "So the best for Comedy amongst vs bee ... Anthony Mundye our best plotter."[10] Nashe, in *Lenten Stuffe* (1599) says, "Is it not right of the merry coblers cutte in that witty play of *The Case Is Altered?*"[11]—a clear allusion to Juniper. Finally, three tiny but recognizable quotations from *The Case Is Altered* are buried in John Bodenham's *Belvedere* (1600). Discovered by C. H. Crawford,[12] these become early "allusions to Jonson" in *The Jonson Allusion-Book* by Bradley and Adams.[13] *Belvedere* has two commendatory poems by Henslowe men, A. Munday and R. Hathway, and "A. M." (presumably Anthony Munday) helped edit the book. The only evidence that these three quotations are from Jonson is the title page of the 1609 quarto. All three are drawn from the plot of the false steward Jacques and his stolen daughter, and could have been proudly culled by Munday as editor of *Beleuedere* from that part of the old play which he himself was primarily responsible for.[14]

Onto a play called *The Case Is Altered* that had already received considerable notice, Jonson, after 1600,[15] grafted the opening scene of Antonio Balladino, clearly a take-off on Anthony Munday. The interpolated character derives his name from "ballad," the form of poetry Munday was famous for, and *Paladine of England*, the title of one of Munday's translated French romances. Balladino is asked by Juniper (1. 2. 14–16) to make Onion "some prety *Paradox* or some *Aligory*," for Onion is in love. In 1593 Munday had published his *Paradoxes*. Balladino confesses that he is "Pageant Poet to the City of *Millaine*" (1. 2., 31–32), one of Munday's appointments to the City of London. Finally he boasts that "the plot shall carry it" (1. 2., 77), but at this point Valentine, the original character, takes back his part in the play and "Balladino" disappears.

Now Valentine as a critic of the theater has been thought[16] to anticipate Asper, Crites, and Horace, famous mouthpieces of Ben Jonson. But Valentine appears in only six scenes, has very little to do with either plot, and temporarily changes his character to that of critic for no apparent artistic reason. In 1. 3, he is recognized, after a long period of travel, as the "poet" Valentine; in the following two scenes he is a traveler and messenger. In 2. 7, cudgels are brought on stage for a bout of fencing. Since Valentine is well-traveled, he is asked about fencing in Utopia, and he replies they do have fencing there. How do they fence? "Marry, first they are brought to the publicke *Theatre*" (2. 7., 26), which gives him an ill-prepared opportunity to criticize the theater audiences in Utopia:

> And they have taken such a habit of dislike in all things, that they will approue nothing, be it neuer so conceited or elaborate, but sit disperst, making faces, and spitting, wagging their vpright eares, and cry filthy, filthy. Simply vttering their owne condition, and vsing their wryed countenances in stead of a vice, to turne the good aspects of all that shall sit neare them, from what they behold [2. 7. 76–82]

A parallel speech occurs in *Every Man Out of His Humour:*

> *Asper.* How monstrous and detested is't, to see
> A fellow, that has neither arts nor braine.
> Sit like an ARTISTARCHVS, or starke-asse,
> Taking mens lines, with a tobacco face,
> In snuffe, still spitting, vsing his wryed lookes
> (In nature of a vice) to wrest, and turne
> The good aspect of those that shall sit neare him,
> From what they doe behold! O, 'tis most vile![17]

Did Jonson write Valentine's speech in *The Case Is Altered?* Jonson's Asper, as his name implies, is a fault-finding critic from first to last; Valentine, a sudden critic in a single scene. What is more, Jonson's critic-characters are never attended by a fool like Juniper who keeps addressing them as "Ningle"—"How now, my sweet ningle?" When Jonson depicts himself as critic he stays "high and aloof," and does not join himself as "ningle" to anyone.[18] In other words, the one actually parallel passage that "proves" Jonson wrote *The Case Is Altered* could have been added by Jonson's rivals to the original play in order to satirize Jonson after the 1600 quarto of *Every Man Out of His Humor.* That Valentine in his brief critic's role is a backlash at Jonson rather than a foretaste of Asper, Crites, or Horace, raises the interesting possibility that the very title of the play invited its use on three different occasions: (1) it was a popular Henslowe play; (2) Jonson's critics rewrote part of Valentine's character to satirize the Jonsonian Asper's criticism of London audiences; (3) Jonson used the same character, this time as "Balladino," to strike back at them, particularly Anthony Munday, so "the case is altered."

Whatever reflections Munday cast on Jonson, they were sufficient to cause Jonson to attack him twice, as the poet Nuntius in *Every Man In* (late 1598) and as Balladino. Jonson had reasons to hate the man.[19] As a Protestant poursuivant he exposed Jesuit priests, and Jonson was a new Roman Catholic. Like Balladino, Munday was a boastful traveler abroad. He was a famous balladist, in Jonson's eyes the extreme of popular magpie poet.[20] Along with Dekker, Chettle, Drayton, Hathway, he was a member of Henslowe's group of dramatists and had collaborated in successful plays. Up to 1598 Jonson had been associated with some of these men; then he was imprisoned for killing Gabriel Spencer in a duel. Henslowe called him "bricklayer" and Jonson gave his next play to the Lord Chamberlain's Men.

Meres had called Munday "our best plotter" in comedy, probably in the sense of concocting new plays from varied and perhaps old materials. And Marston in *Histriomastix* (1598/9) has Gulch cap a quotation from Munday with "Heer's no new luxury or blandishment. / But plenty of old Englands mothers / Words."[21] *The Case Is Altered* is just such a play as Meres and Marston describe. Its extreme brevity may be another reason for thinking it not by Jonson, whose known plays are approximately one-third longer; *The Case Is Altered* and Munday's *John a Kent* are both very brief by contemporary standards.

Everybody knew about the poets' quarrel and Jonson's name was the most famous in it. Perhaps his last connection with it was the Antonio Balladino joke. Jonson quit. Years later, *The Case Is Altered* with Jonson's opening scene was revived by the Children of the Blackfriars, a title not conferred upon that company until about 1606.[22] In 1609 two enterprising booksellers, Bartholomew Sutton and William Barrenger, published it as "Written by Ben. Ionson," a sure hit. But Ben Jonson repudiated it not because it was a bad play of his early apprenticeship (Selin), not because he had refurbished *Every Man In* and *Every Many Out* to fit his critical theory and therefore suppressed what did not fit (Enck); but, more simply, because it was never Jonson's intention to lay claim to what was not his.

This hypothesis satisfies the known facts of the history of *The Case Is Altered*. It accounts for the revival of the play not on grounds of intrinsic excellence but by joining it to the poets' quarrel. It suggests a reason for Jonson's choosing this play to pillory Anthony Munday in; and it makes sense out of the grafting of Balladino onto the character Valentine. As with all our "essays in persuasion," however, so here, the case for Jonson's authorship, or for Anthony Munday's, or for anybody else's,[23] cannot, with certainty, be proved.

4   *Macbeth* and the Jesuit Priest

The drunken porter in *Macbeth* says: "Faith, here's an equivocator, that could swear in both the scales against either
scale; who has committed treason enough for God's sake, yet
could not equivocate to heaven. O, come in, equivocator" (2. 3).
Shakespeare's eighteenth-century editor, Bishop Warburton, glos-
sed the term "equivocator" as "a Jesuit; an order so troublesome
in Queen Elizabeth's and King James the First's time." And he
referred to "the invention of the execrable doctrine of equivocation." While Londoners were flocking to opening night of Shakespeare's *Macbeth*, the following typical interrogation was being
repeated in many a courtroom:

> JUDGE: "Have you sworn by Almighty God to tell the
> truth?"
> JESUIT: "I have, your Honor."
> JUDGE: "Are you a priest?"
> JESUIT: "Your Honor, I swear by Almighty God that I am
> not a priest [of Apollo]".

The phrase in square brackets was never spoken. This kind of
deliberate holding back part of "the whole truth" was known as

This argument was initially read at the Newberry Library conference in
Chicago in April 1963 and was published in *PMLA* 79 (1964): 390–400; I
have gratefully incorporated corrections by W. Malloch in *PMLA* 80
(1965). Anxious about the tone of my treatment of the Society of Jesus, for
which I have great respect, I sent the article to my friend Father Walter J.
Ong, S.J., of Saint Louis. He gave it his blessing.

"Jesuitical equivocation." Throughout the tragedy, parts of the truth are withheld: at the beginning the hero does not divulge in his letter to his wife the witches' prophecy of Banquo's issue; and at the end, we are not allowed to read the letters that Lady Macbeth in her sleep writes, folds, and seals. Jesuitical equivocation was in the public mind during and after the trial and execution for treason of Father Garnett, S.J., for complicity in the Gunpowder Plot of 5 November 1605.[1]

It was clearly defined by the presiding judge, Sir Edward Coke, at that trial on 28 March 1606. Of the Jesuits Coke said:

> Their dissimulation appeareth out of their doctrine of equivocation. [There is] the treatise of equivocation, seen and allowed by Garnett . . .; wherein, under the pretext of the lawfulness of a mixt proposition to express one part of a man's mind, and retain another, people are indeed taught, not only simple lying, but fearful and damnable blasphemy.[2]

Father Garnett was found guilty and sentenced to be hanged, drawn, and quartered. In a letter of 2 May 1606, Sir Dudley Carleton prophesied: "He will equivocate at the gallows; but he will be hanged without equivocation."[3] Next day he was hanged, but at the express command of King James he was allowed to hang until he was dead, a recommendation of mercy, since Father Garnett was a learned, pious, and important man. Despite the fact that the trial was hardly a model of legal procedure even by the standards of the day, to practically every Englishman there was no doubt that Father Garnett was an equivocator who had "committed treason enough for God's sake." Leslie Hotson has reminded us how close Shakespeare was to the men, the places, and the stirred-up feelings of the Gunpowder Plot.[4]

The doctrine of equivocation seems to have begun with Martin d'Azpilcueta, professor of canon law at Rome, called Navarrus because he came from Navarre.[5] It is part of systematic casuistry, moral theology that treats of cases of conscience. At one point Navarrus recounts an incident in the life of Saint Francis of Assisi. When the constabulary were chasing a poor wretch suspected of robbery they asked Francis, "Did you see the thief? Which way did he go?" Francis, placing his hands in his sleeves, pointed with a hidden finger in the right direction but looking in the opposite direction said, "He went that way." Impelled by charity, Saint

Francis told the truth in the sight of God, though of course the police never caught their man.[6]

The *Treatise of Equivocation* that hanged Father Garnett is one of the Laudian manuscripts in the Bodleian Library.[7] On its cover in Coke's hand are these words: "This Booke, containing 61 pages, I founde in a Chamber in the Inner Temple, wherein Sir Thomas Tresham used to lye. This 5 of December, 1605." It was evidently written by Garnett to help defend his friend and coworker Robert Southwell, S.J., who was executed in 1595, and is dedicated to his martyred spirit. The treatise begins with Saint Jerome's threefold criteria for every oath: truth, discretion, and justice.[8] Truth and falsehood characterize enunciative propositions, and Aristotle admits these may be spoken or written or thought or mixed. A mixed proposition can be spoken and written, spoken and thought, or written and thought.[9] For example, a dying man could say before witnesses to his heir, "I bequeath to you, my son," then his voice failing, write with the pen thrust into his hand, "1,000 florins." This spoken and written proposition would stand up in any court. Thus the answer, "I am not a priest [of Apollo]," which mixes spoken and thought segments, is not a lie. Thought precedes speaking, and God knows my mind.

The best printed defense of the Jesuitical doctrine of equivocation was published by Robert Parsons, S.J.: *A Treatise tending to Mitigation towards the Catholike Subjects in England . . . against Bishop Thomas Morton's two slanderous grounds of rebellion and equivocation* (London, 1607).[10] After a long historical introduction, Parsons asks his adversary the famous "bloody question," which can be paraphrased thus: "Suppose our gracious King were being sought out by brigands and coming upon you, Thomas Morton, Bishop of Durham, they ask, 'Where is the King? We are sent to murder him.' How would you answer? If you tell a lie, you offend God. If you tell the truth, you become accessory to the murder of your Sovereign. You must equivocate by saying, '*Nescio* [*ut te dicam*]—I know not [to the end of telling you].' To be sure this deludes the murderers, but the whole proposition to God who can read your mind is a true one; the men sentencing His Majesty have no jurisdiction; your equivocation saves the King's life and incidentally your own soul."

William Cecil Lord Burghley had devised the "bloody question" in the early 1580s. Speaking of the Roman Catholics, he wrote:

And at their arraignement, when they laboured to leaue in the minds of the people, and standers by an opinion that they were to dye, not for treason, but for matter of faith and conscience in doctrine, touching the seruice of God, without any attempt or purpose against her Maiestie, they cried out, that they were true subiects, and did, and woulde obey and serue her Maiestie. Immediately, to proue whether that hypocriticall and sophistical speach extended to a perpetuitie of their obedience, or to so long time as the Pope permitted, or not, they were openly, in place of judgement, asked by the Queene's learned counsell, whether they woulde obey, and be true subiectes, if the Pope commanded the contrary? They plainly disclosed themselves in answers, saying by the mouth of Campion, this place (meaning the court of her Maiesties bench) hath no power to enquire, or judge of the holy fathers authorities; and other answer they would not make.[11]

The Jesuitical answer to the "bloody question," emerging from a series of trials for treason, was "Were the Pope to send an army to invade England, we would be on the side of Our Gracious Sovereign Queen Elizabeth [if the Pope so commanded]." As Thomas Bell wrote in 1603, two years before the Gunpowder Plot, by virtue of the doctrine of equivocation, "The Iesuites take pleasure to forge and inuent things that are not, so that now a dayes they are commonly holden for great lyars; & it is come to passe that though they sweare, men will not beleeue them."[12]

The devil, equivocation, treason, and the murdering of Protestant kings is the whole burden, right or wrong, of the political and legal debate over the Jesuits that preceded and followed Shakespeare's *Macbeth*. Shakespeare begins with the assumption that equivocation springs from the devil and that, in the Christian view of order, the devil is the archtraitor. Macbeth is introduced as a brave soldier, commended by his sovereign for loyally stamping out a treasonous rebellion. Meeting the witches, who, as King James well knew, are in league with the devil, he is seduced by their technical equivocation, and through his wife's evil strength and his own moral weakness, ends by becoming its victim.

The Jesuits, asserting their belief that God and his vicegerent at Rome are above the king, placed their religious loyalty above their political. The witches owe their allegiance not to God but to the devil. If it came to a showdown with them whether they would choose the devil or the king, of course they would choose the devil. In this form of witch treason (James himself had had experience with witch treason in the Dr. Fian affair) the witches would equivocate as the Jesuits did, and for the same reason: that of asserting the higher power over the lower. Hence, although the initial prophecies of the witches in *Macbeth* can be taken as mere amphibology, they may also, given the political background, be taken as technical equivocation. Their propositions are true with mental reservation: (1) to Macbeth—"You will be king [if you are willing to commit murder];" (2) to Banquo—"Your children will be kings [if Macbeth murders Duncan and you but not Fleance]." At the end of the play Macbeth discovers that the wtiches' prophecies are "th' equivocation of the fiend, that lies like truth" (5, 5, 43) a description of the doctrine that echoes the denunciations in the pamphlet war we have just reviewed.

Apparently Macbeth has already entertained treasonous thoughts before he meets the witches (cf. 1. 3., 149–50, and 1. 7., 47–55). His mind readily takes the spoken half of their propositions for he truth that he will act upon. The hidden parts, however, which make up "the whole truth," work upon his conscience:

> My thought, whose murther is yet but fantastical,
> Shakes so my single state of man
> That function is smother'd in surmise,
> And nothing is, but what is not.
>
> [1. 3., 139–42]

Banquo, the more forthright, knows that, by hiding information, "the devil can speak true" and not true simultaneously:

> . . . oftentimes, to win us to our harm,
> The instruments of Darkness tell us truths;
> Win us with honest trifles, to betray's
> In deepest consequence.
>
> [1. 3., 123–26]

Lady Macbeth is damned from her very first appearance because she can read between the lines of her husband's apparently factual report: she knows that her husband is determining already "To catch the nearest way" to the crown and she fears his milk-white nature. The witches, therefore, by indirection have already made this equivocal speech to Lady Macbeth: "You can help your husband be king [if you are willing to be damned for intuitively arriving at the knowledge which we and the fiend alone fully possess, i.e., that Duncan will be murdered by Macbeth]." Such action-propositions involve two times: the present, which is the dilemma, and that future or no-time which belongs to the higher power. Among the Jesuits that higher power was God; in this husband and wife it is the devil's already accomplished will. Lady Macbeth expresses it well when she welcomes her husband with "Thy letters have transported me beyond / This ignorant present, and I feel now / The future in the instant" (1. 5., 56–58)—a diabolical twist on the insight that must come to a martyr at the moment that he grasps fully what God's purpose for him is: the point where the two times meet. Absolute truth, one would suppose, would be the identity of the thing and the thought and the utterance. But equivocation, as we have seen, is a device to gain time by splitting the times of an action proposition, as in this example beginning with *Dabo*: "I will give you half my winnings [if I win five hundred dollars in the third race]." Macbeth finally discovers the logical ruse:

> And be these juggling fiends no more believ'd
> That palter with us in a double sense;
> That keep the word of promise to our ear,
> And break it to our hope.
>
> [5. 7., 20–23]

All the undivulged, kept-back, secret conditions on which final truth must hang keep crowding forward; it is they which afflict Lady Macbeth beyond a mere physician's care:

> Cure her of that:
> Canst thou not minister to a mind *diseas'd,*
> Pluck from the memory of a rooted sorrow,
> *Raze* out the *written* troubles of the brain,
> And with some sweet oblivious antidote
> Cleanse the stuff'd bosom of that perilous stuff
> Which weighs upon the *heart?*
>
> [5. 3., 39–45, my italics]

Equivocation leads to treason in that it holds back mentally one-half of a proposition in order to delude the hearer by that half which is spoken. This is the definition Banquo gives it:

> Fear and scruples shake us:
> In the great hand of God I stand; and thence
> Against the *undivulg'd* pretence I fight
> Of treasonous malice,
>
> [2. 3., 129–32, my italics]

when Banquo appeals to God's ability to read a human mind and thus to judge the unspoken part of any treasonous proposition.

Treason springs from a more intense loyalty to a higher command, who speaks not in words but to the mind. In the plan of treason not once do we have a twinge of conscience from Lady Macbeth; she is "the fiend-like queen" (very end of the play). It is she who urges her husband to fulfill the unheard portions of the witches' true propositions. As in the fall of man, it is the woman who takes the devil's initial idea and teaches it to the man, who thereafter becomes not the pupil but the master. Macbeth again practices the art of equivocation with the one person who loves him by keeping back half of a proposition that involves a second murder. Banquo and Fleance are still alive. Macbeth has just given orders for their murder, equivocating with his hired assassins by *not* telling them of the third murderer. To his wife he vouchsafes only a general hint of a "deed of dreadful note," then says, "There's comfort yet." "What's to be done?" Lady Macbeth enquires. "Be innocent of the knowledge, dearest chuck," he replies (3. 2., 39–46). Truth must consist of both heart and tongue, and the whole truth is not there when half of it is kept within.

When Macbeth meets the witches again he urges upon himself the unuttered part of their prophecies. His first meeting was accidental, but at this meeting he demands and forces the omens of darkness to speak. With proud recklessness he takes only that half of their true propositions which he hears: (1) no man born of woman can harm you, Macbeth [not counting a Caesarian section]; (2) you will not be vanquished till Birnam Woods move to Dunsinane [omitting of course the exigencies of military camouflage]. By this time, treasonous equivocation which is not the whole truth has turned the world of value upside down. Macbeth is a traitor to the king; but when Macbeth becomes king, then all those forces of righteousness against him become "traitors."

Macbeth at last realizes the equivocation which is the key to his own tragedy to consist of the discrepancy between the words of the mouth and the meditations of the heart, a discrepancy whose deliberate and foolhardy cultivation for an evil end isolates him from the rest of humanity:

> That which should accompany old age,
> As honour, love, obedience, troops of friends,
> I must not look to have; but in their stead,
> Curses, not loud but deep, *mouth-honour*, breath,
> Which the poor *heart* would fain deny, and dare not
> [5. 3., 24–28, my italics]

—an echo of Isaiah 29:13, "This people draw near me with their mouth, and with their lips do honour me, but have removed their heart far from me."

Shakespeare sustains the tragic irony by allowing deliberately concealed propositions of treason to be flushed into the open with streams of innocent and guilty blood. The background of Jesuitical equivocation, publicly discussed as a doctrine of the devil for the murdering of kings, lends political, psychological, ethical, and even religious realism to Macbeth's treasonous dissimulations. The traitor and king-murderer dies with his armor on, fighting as Robert Catesby did, the gunpowder conspirator, with no equivocation at the gallows. Were he to confess his treason in *words*, who would believe him now?

Macbeth is a tragic figure because, caught by his own toils in "the bloody question," he has to die: "Macbeth, if the devil told you to murder the king, and God said, 'No,' would you be on the devil's side or on that of God and the king?" His answer was: "I would take God's side and the king's [*if the devil so commanded*]." The drunken porter welcomes his equivocator to an imagined hell, and with horror we watch Macbeth enter it almost against his will.

5   King James as Solomon, the Book of Proverbs, and Hall's *Characters*

Character writing, like casuistry, is a peculiarly seventeenth-century literary phenomenon, and the vogue began in England with Joseph Hall's *Characters of Vertues and Vices*, published in 1608.[1] The ancient Greek Theophrastus was the father, hardly known in modern Europe until Isaac Casaubon published his edition of the "characters" in 1591, followed by a meticulous commentary. Hall's *Characters*, however, are un-Theophrastan in their addition of "vertuous" portraits to the "vicious," in their general lack of humor, and in their emphasis upon the Christian religion. Although for years it has been the custom to make parallels between Hall and his Greek "source,"[2] the great difference exists. Various theories have attempted to accommodate it, the most popular one being that Ben Jonson's "humours" are the real beginning of the English "character."[3]

Fifty-five years ago, however, Richard Aldington made an interesting conjecture "for anyone to verify or refute" that "we owe the sudden vogue of character-writing in England to King James."[4] The purpose of this essay is to persuade my readers that Aldington was right.

Obnoxious though James I was in his pedantic egoism, his phobias, guile, and self-indulgence[5], Joseph Hall had an almost sycophantic esteem for the man. As a nineteen-year-old student at Cambridge, he wrote an "eclogue," now lost, welcoming the birth

This essay is recast from chapter 4 of my book *Bishop Joseph Hall (1574–1656: A Biographical and Critical Study* (Cambridge: D. S. Brewer, 1979).

in Scotland of Prince Henry.[6] To lament the death of Elizabeth and celebrate the succession of James I, Hall published *The King's Prophecy; or, Weeping Joy* (1603), a 384-line poem of almost unrestrained enthusiasm for the Scottish king. In the next two years, chafing under the narrow confines and low salary of the chaplaincy in Sir Robert Drury's household in Suffolk, Hall published two religious books and had decided to become a churchman under the establishment. As Providence worked out, his *Meditations and Vowes* (1605) simultaneously caught the attention of Baron Edward Denny of Waltham and of young Prince Henry at Nonesuch. The following year Hall was called to Waltham Holy Cross as rector at ten times his former salary, and was asked by the prince to become one of his twenty-four personal chaplains, to serve, as the procedure was, two at a time for one month each year.

At Waltham, only twelve miles from the center of England's political and ecclesiastical power, Hall wrote and preached for the next twenty years. His first book written in these congenial and glowing surroundings was the *Characters*, dedicated to "the right honourable my singular good lords" Edward Lord Denny and his son-in-law James Lord Hay, the latter so much a favorite at court that James made him Lord Doncaster and finally Earl of Carlisle. In his autobiography Hall speaks from experience of the king's custom at mealtime, witnessed by many others, of inviting a few of his favorite preachers to stand behind his chair and parry his theological questions (in Latin) while His Majesty ate.

James brought to the British throne a learning that extended from prosody to theology, a reading knowledge of Latin, Greek, and Hebrew, an unusual skill in disputation, and an ability to speak fluently, if with a Scottish accent, Latin, French, and English. Among his favorite books in the Bible were the three ascribed to Solomon: the Canticles, the Proverbs, and Ecclesiastes, written, as tradition had it, in Solomon's young manhood, in his middle age, and toward the end of his life. In *Basilikon Doron* (1599), addressed like the book of Proverbs, to "my son" (see Prov. 1:8), Scotland's "Solomon" advises the six-year old Prince Henry as follows:

> Reade . . . the books of the *Proverbes* & *Ecclesiastes*, written by that great patterne of wisdome Salomon: whiche will not onlie serue you for instruction, how to walke in the obedience of the Lawe of God, but is also so full of golden

sentences, & morall precepts, in all things that can con-
cerne your conversations in the worlde, as amonge all the
prophane Philosophers and Poets, ye shall not find so rich
a storehouse of precepts of naturall wisedome, agreeing
with the will & Diuine wisdome of God.[7]

James divides the whole of Christian teaching into two antithetical parts: a command to do good and a prohibition against
evil. "Remember also," he continues, "that by the right knowledge, and feare of God (whiche is the *beginning of wisdome*, as
Salomon saith) ye shall know all the things necessary for the dis-
charge of your duety, both as a Christian & as a king" (p. 27).

On style, James is very explicit:

In both your speaking and gesture, vse a naturall and
plaine forme, not fairded with artifice: for (as the French
men say) *Rien contrefaict fin:* but eschewe all affectate
formes in both. In your language be plaine, honest, naturall, comelie, cleane, short, and sentencious: eschewing
both the extremities, as well as in not vsing any rusticall
corrupt leide, as booke-language, and pen and inke-horne
tearmes: and least of all mignarde & effoeminate termes.
But let the greatest parte of your eloquence consiste in a
natural, cleare, and sensible forme of the deliuerie of your
minde.... Now as to your writing, whiche is nothing
else, but a forme of enregistrate speeche, vse a plaine,
shorte, but statelie stile. [Pp. 179–80, 183]

In his own behavior James deliberately followed his great predecessor in a wish for an understanding heart (1 Kings 3:9–15); in
the making of wise decisions (1 Kings 3:16–28); in choosing and
properly elevating his wife as the Queen of Sheba (1 Kings
10:1–10); in keeping peace with neighboring nations, and in en-
listing the aid of clever foreigners (1 Kings 5). Well known is the
story of James settling a quarrel during his progress southward in
1603: two English courtiers were about to fight over who should
have the honor of carrying the new king's sword, so James quietly
gave it to a neutral third man. That the original two were satisfied
evoked a universal memory of the biblical wise king, a quarrel-
some pair, and a sword (1 Kings 3:16–28).

Throughout his reign panegyrical speeches, dedications, and
sermons constantly compared King James and King Solomon.
William Barlow fulsomely dedicated his account of the Hampton

Court conference to James with many a parallel to Solomon, particularly in respect to their speech: "words as they are uttered by him, being as Solomon speaketh, like apples of gold, with pictures of silver" (Prov. 25:11, Geneva).[8] In the first year of the new reign, to welcome Queen Anne's brother, King Christian IV of Denmark, Robert Cecil first Earl of Salisbury put on a show at Theobalds (before he traded that sumptuous house to the king on royal demand) in imitation of "King Solomon's Temple." As the court lady representing the Queen of Sheba rose to present the visiting monarch with a cornucopia of fruit, she vomited in his lap; and James himself, attempting to dance with her, fell to the floor from attempting to keep pace bowl for bowl with Denmark.[9] The story, told by Sir John Harrington, is hilarious, spiteful, and sad, but the important point is that in 1604 Cecil chose the Solomonic stage setting for his masque.

On 30 April 1605 a sermon was preached before the king at Nonesuch by the Reverend Robert Wakeman entitled "Solomon's Exaltation." John Carpenter dedicated to James his *Schelomonecham; or, King Solomon his Solace* (1606) with dozens of parallels between the two kings, including the fact that both were "brief in their sentences," and both were the authors of a "booke of sapience." Bishop George Carleton of Chichester, in *A Thankful Remembrance of Gods Mercy* (1624), reviews recent English history in providential terms, and notes that Elizabeth was "succeeded [by] our peaceable *Solomon*, King James" (p. 176).

Joseph Hall admired in his sovereign two of Solomon's traits: wisdom and peacekeeping. On James's erudition he said in his sermon before the king to celebrate the tenth anniversary of his accession: "Let me begin with that which the heathen man required to the happiness of any state, his learning and knowledge: wherein I may safely say, he exceedeth all his one hundred and five predecessors.... What king christened hath written so learned volumes?"[10] And in a sermon entitled "The true Peace maker," preached before His Majesty at Theobalds on 19 September 1624, Hall quotes "wise Solomon's" sayings: "'The crown of the wise is their riches: but the foolishness of fooles is folly'" (Prov. 14:24, AV); and "'When a man's wayes please the Lord, he maketh even his enemies to be at peace with him'" (Prov. 16: 7, AV). Hall ends his sermon with this: "What good hath the earth which God doth not couch under the name of peace? Blessed be

God and his anointed, we have long and comfortably tasted the sweetnesse of his blessing. The lilies and lions of our Solomon have been justly worded with *Beati pacifici*" (5:230)—an allusion to James's royal coat of arms. It is not unlikely that Hall had King James in mind when he ended his "character" of "The Good Magistrate" with: "He is the Guard of good laws, the Refuge of Innocency, the Comet of the guilty, the Paymaster of good deserts, the Champion of justice, the Patron of peace, the Tutor of the Church, the Father of his Country, &, as it were, another God vpon earth."

The sedulously cultivated image of James as Solomon could fill a book, but we must hasten to its end, the sermon preached at his funeral on 7 May 1625, entitled "Great Britain's Solomon" by Bishop John Williams of Lincoln. The three texts of 1 Kings 11:41, 42, and 43 divide the sermon into the life, the reign, and the death of the two kings. In their lives they both praised eloquence as a kingly virtue, performed great *acta* to match their *verba*, and became models of wisdom. Surely the bishop's list of similarities is exhaustive: both kings were only sons; both were infant kings (James at thirteen months); both had white and ruddy complexions; both rose above serious difficulties at the beginnings of their reigns; both wrote eloquent prose and poetry. Of England's dead king, Bishop Williams concluded: "In his *Style* you may observe the *Ecclesiastes*, in his *Figures* the *Canticles*, in his Sentences the *Proverbs*, and in his whole *Discourse, Reliquiem verborum Solomonis*, all the rest that was admirable in the Eloquence of Salomon."

James's Solomonic reputation for wisdom continued in a macabre note on his being embalmed for burial: "The semyture of his head soe stronge as that they could hardly breake it open with a chissell and sawe, and so full of braynes as they could not, uppon the openning, keepe them from spillinge, a great marke of his infinite judgement."[11]

Solomon's two leading antithetical terms combined in a witty paradox ensure that King James go down in history as "the wisest fool in Christendom."[12] A more charitable, because self-chosen, memorial is the great ceiling painted by Rubens on commission for the Whitehall banqueting house, finally delivered to Charles I in 1635. James built Whitehall for his great state occasions, and he had made contact with Rubens as early as 1619.[13] The large central painting depicts James as Solomon leaning forward in his throne,

pointing with his scepter (like a sword) at two ample female figures (England and Scotland) wrestling over a male child (Prince
Charles) while attempting to place on his head parts of two
crowns. Minerva (Wisdom) stands behind binding the crowns together with an iron band at the command of the king, while two
winged *putti* carry above her head the emblazoned escutcheon of
the new era of PEACE. Thus James claimed for posterity his Old
Testament "type." The first mark of his peaceful reign had been
the union by proclamation of Scotland and England.

Now Hall's admiration for James's pacifism, learning, and sententious style may well have impelled him to restudy the books in
the Bible ascribed to the king's adopted model. In 1609 there appeared under the name of "Jos. Hall" *Solomon's Divine Arts, of 1.
Ethics: 2. Politics: 3. Economics. That is The Government of 1. Behaviour: 2. Commonwealth: 3. Family. Drawne into Method Out Of
his Proverbs and Ecclesiastes.* Though this biblical work was published a year after the *Characters,* the two were registered the same
year: the *Characters* on 7 March 1608 and *Solomon's Divine Arts* on 8
December 1608. Given the lightness of the *Characters* and the den-
sity of Hall's concordance—evidence of the research and pains
required for its composition—I have no doubt that while writing
the *Characters* Hall was deeply involved in Solomon's ethical wisdom, especially as it emerges in the Book of Proverbs.

Dedicating the book to Robert Earl of Essex, who in 1606 had
conveyed to Hall Prince Henry's invitation, Hall refers to Solomon
as "the royalest philosopher and wisest king," a description James
no doubt applied to himself. Hall's method is to make a concordance of Solomon's wise sayings, placing them under certain
heads for the easier finding. His initial division, *ethical behavior,*
is subdivided into *end* and *means*. The end is *felicity*, which is
found only in obeying God's commands. The means to that felicity
are *prudence* (being wise in God's commands), *justice, temperance,*
and *fortitude*. Throughout, the virtues quoted and paraphrased
from the Geneva Bible are balanced with their opposites, as they
are in *Characters of Vertues and Vices*. This disjunctive habit of mind
is Ramistic in its reliance upon the either/or dichotomy. Embraced
by Continental Reformed theologians, the method was brought to
Glasgow University by the great Scottish Calvinist Andrew Mel-
ville, and later was taught at Cambridge, mainly at Hall's own
college, Emmanuel. In the very first sentence of *Solomon's Divine*

Arts, Hall takes his definition of ethics from Ecclesiastes 1:17: "And I gaue mine heart to knowe wisdome & knowledge, madnes & foolishnes" (Geneva). Since felicity is the end of wisdom, Hall defines it (*a*) negatively and (*b*) positively. To define "virtue" he tells us (*a*) what it is and (*b*) how it is ruled. For "discretion" he discovers from Solomon (*a*) what it is and (*b*) how it works; it works *either* in our actions *or* in our speech (8:213), etc.

As readers of the Bible have known for a long time, Proverbs itself contains rudimentary "characters," like "the glutton is...," "The wrathful man stirreth...," The slothful man sayeth," "A faithful man shall abound with blessings," etc. Several longer "characters" emerge in the twenty-sixth chapter: The Fool (1–12), The Sluggard (13–16), The Trouble-Maker (17–22), and The Hypocrite (23–8). The most sustained "character" in Proverbs is A Vertuous Woman in the 'final chapter as part of the consistent hypostatization of wisdom. Opposite her are The Harlot (7: 6–27) and A Foolish Woman (9:13–18).

To pass from content to style, warned by Harold Fisch's important article "The Limits of Hall's Senecanism,"[14] we are reminded that Hall could read in Hebrew those poetic parts of the Old Testament written in distichs of three kinds: (1) synonymous, in which the two elements are identical in meaning; (2) antithetical, in which they are contrary; and (3) a combination of the two.[15] Two examples of synonymy ascribed to Solomon and thus appearing in Hall's concordance are Ecclesiastes 1:18 "For in the multitude of wisdome is muche grief: & he that encreaseth knowledge, encreaseth sorrowe"; and Proverbs 9:10—"The beginning of wisdom is the feare of the Lord, & the knowledge of holy things is vnderstanding" (quoted by King James to his son Henry). The most antithetical chapter of Proverbs, on the other hand, is the tenth: each of its thirty-two verses (AV) consists of two parallel statements connected with the adversative conjunction "but." Thus a not unexpected characteristic of Hall's book on Solomon's wisdom is his constant use of the word "contrarily" (for example, pp. 227, 228, 239, 249, 250, 258, 254, etc.) to define virtues in terms of vices and vices in terms of virtues.

Hall's *Characters of Vertues & Vices* is very similar, in its oppositions and constant reminder that wisdom is to be found in worshiping God. The Faithful Man of the *Characters* is Fidelity in *Solomon's Divine Arts.* Its opposite is the hypocrite and the flatterer in Proverbs, which become two of Hall's Vices. Hall continues (p.

238) from the Book of Proverbs with the dissembler as being "vainglorious," "impenitent," "envious," "prodigal," and "slothful"—each one of these five opposites finding its place among his "Characters of Vices." Also, Fortitude in Solomon's wisdom parallels the Valiant Man in *Characters*, and Hall's account of Solomonic "temperance" (pp. 246–48) includes Humility and Patience, virtues that correspond with the Humble Man and the Patient Man in the *Characters*. Wisdom, with which he starts the virtues, rests firmly on reason upheld by religion.

All the virtues that follow center not on morality but on God. For example, "If [the honest man] see what he must doe, let God see what shall follow" (p. 150). The whole of the character of the Faithful Man is an account of his relationship to God: "He is allied so high, that hee dare call God Father, his Saviour Brother: heaven his Patrimony, and thinkes it no presumption to trust to the attendance of Angels" (p. 151). When the humble man "approcheth to the Throne of God, he is so taken up with the divine greatnesse, that in his owne eyes he is either vile or nothing" (p. 153). The Valiant Man is "afraid of nothing but the displeasure of the Highest, and runs away from nothing but sin" (p. 154). "Gods best witness" is the Patient Man (p. 155), and the True Friend is motivated by "the best of vertues, Religion" (p. 156). The Truly-Noble man "is more carefull to give true honour to his Maker, then to receive civill honour from men" (p. 159), while "The Good Magistrate . . . is the faithful Deputy of his Maker, whose obedience is the rule whereby he ruleth" (p. 160). Surely David's "broken and contrite heart" for sins committed defines Hall's the Penitent Man, the longest of the characters, for "Hee is a thankfull Herauld of the mercies of his God" (p. 163). At last, the Happy Man, which Hall added to his second edition in 1614, is happy because "He keeps ever the best company, the God of Spirits and the Spirits of that God" (p. 166). Thus, as wisdom begins the virtues, felicity ends them—both in God.[16]

The denial of God gives rise to the vices, and not one of them can possibly be "happy"; they are all Malcontents. Not only is vice the opposite of virtue but individual vices are demonstrably set against individual virtues. As the fool is the opposite of the wise in Solomon's book, so in Hall's *Characters* the final virtue, happiness, is deliberately added in opposition to the final vice, envy: "Whatsoever God doe for [the envious man] he cannot be happy with company; and if he were to chuse, whether he would rather have equals in a common felicitie or superiours in misery, hee would demurre upon the election" (p. 195). Several vices oppose the virtuous Faithful Man: the Distrustful Man, the Prophane Man (who worships no God), and the Superstitious Man (who worships many gods). Both the Hypocrite and the Flatterer are the opposite of the Honest Man, whereas the Presumptous Man is the opposite of the Humble. The antithesis of the Patient Man is the Busie-bodie. Finally, Hall's Truly-Noble Man is opposed by such vicious characters as the slothful, the covetous, the ambitious, and the envious—all of whom, like the last one named, are "enemies to Gods favours" (p. 197).

It is not surprising, then, that the first book of "characters" in England, written so soon after Hall had been admitted to the court of "England's Solomon," should stem more from Jerusalem than from Athens. In its dedication, Hall refers to Theophrastus, and in all likelihood King James had talked to Hall about Casaubon or possibly lent him the book. We do not know. According to Mark Pattison, "Even in 1601, Casaubon was sufficiently well known to be sought out by foreigners of curiosity who visited Paris." Spotswood, later archbishop of Glasgow, told Casaubon that his learning and piety were well known to James VI. From Edinburgh the monarch wrote an invitational letter "to his dearest Casaubon, telling him that, besides the care of the church, it was his fixed resolve to encourage letters and learned men, as he considered them the strength, as well as the ornament of kingdoms."[17] Just as in *Heaven upon Earth* (1605) Hall as a Christian went "beyond Seneca," so he says "To the Reader" of his *Characters:* "It is no shame for us to learne wit of Heathens; neither is it materiall, in whose schoole we take out a good lesson: yea, it is more shame not to follow their good, than not to lead them better. As one therefore that in worthy examples hold imitation better than invention, I have trod in their paths, but with an higher & wider step." (pp. 143–44).

The religious content, the insistent use of antithetical pairs, and the brief sententious style differentiate Hall's *Characters* from those of his classical predecessor. All three traits are found in the biblical books said to have been written by Solomon, and all three were embraced by King James. The first "character" in Hall's book is the Wise Man.

6 World Harmony, John Donne, and Alexander Pope

One of the reasons why we need art is that it makes a harmony out of the discordant elements in the world and in ourselves. Calling this concept *concors discordia* or *discordia concors*, the ancients described two ways nature harmonizes its own conflicts. One pattern, that of Empedocles, insists upon the balance between fission and fusion; the other, Platonic and Christian, more daringly combines a lower and higher value to achieve a third, which is a systasis of the two.[1] The difference between the poetry of the earlier seventeenth century and that of the eighteenth is that Donne and the "metaphysicals" in their imitation of world harmony are Platonic-Christian, whereas Denham, Dryden, and Pope are Empedoclean and "classical." Dr. Johnson, writing his "Life of Cowley"[2] in the eighteenth century, observed that the metaphysicals were "imitating" *discordia concors* but he did not approve of their "violently yoking" discordant elements together; in his own "Vanity of Human Wishes" he balanced them, as did Empedocles.

Empedocles saw the whole of nature divided between love and hatred and yet held in a stasis among four elements and four qualities. Fire opposes water, and air is set against earth; but fire and air join in their dryness against the juncture by moisture of earth and water. Again, air and water share coldness, which is

Parts of this essay comprised a paper read before the Midwest Modern Language Association at Cincinnati in October 1968, which was published as "Dr. Johnson and Metaphysical Wit; or, *Discordia Concors* Yoked and Balanced," in *Poetic Theory / Poetic Practice*, Papers of the Midwest MLA (Iowa City, Iowa, 1969), pp. 103–12.

balanced and opposed by the fusion through heat of fire and earth.
Thus four elements are balanced by four qualities, and within each
set two pairs are opposed and joined by another two pairs.[3]

Similarly among the four humors and four temperaments in
biology, the sanguine is antithetical to melancholy, and the
choleric to the phlegmatic. And yet two opposed temperaments
are fast while the other two are slow; two are volatile whereas the
other two are calm. The built-in elements and qualities of nature
and of man, then, oppose and join not only philosophically but in
the very pattern of their arrangement.

In a context of the creation of the universe, the ancients used the
phrase *discors concordia,* thus Ovid:

> . . . vapor unidus omnes
> Res creat, et discors concordia, fetibus apta est.[4]

The English Augustan version of this classical idea appeared as
*Ovid's Metamorphoses in Fifteen Books, Translated by the Most Emi-
nent Hands.* (London: J. Tonson, 1717), among which are those of
Dryden, Addison, Congreve, and Gay. The most exact precedent
for Johnson's phrase *discordia concors* occurs in the *Astronomicon* of
the Roman poet Manilius, whom A. E. Housman spent a good part
of his life editing. "Spiritus aut solidus, sitque haec discordia concors," Manilius says (1. 142), and Housman notes the meaning as
identical with that of Empedocles and Ovid.[5] Thus one ancient
classical pattern of *concordia discors* described by Empedocles,
Ovid, and the eminently Augustan Manilius, was thought to have
been put into nature from its foundation, and it is this which the
classical poet, then, is to imitate.

So Virgil, the perfect type of the controlled poet in antiquity,
divided his poems, as Otis Brooks has so admirably demonstrated, into twos, like the Iliadic and Odyssean halves of the
Aeneid, or into fours by means of correlative and antithetical pairs.[6]
Thus of the four *Georgics,* two are concerned with planting and
two with breeding. Of the first two, one describes the planting of
grains, which are small, and the other the planting of trees, which
are large. The last two *Georgics,* both on breeding, oppose each
other in a parallel and chiastic manner: number 3 describes the
breeding of farm animals, which are large, and number 4 discerns
the procreation of bees, which are small. The Virgilian kinds of
poetic fission and fusion here are multitudinous and complex, but

this is sufficient to illustrate the classical, and the neoclassical, ideal of balance through combinations of like and unlike to achieve a *concordia discors* similar to the demiurge's four elements and four qualities.

The eighteenth century is not called Augustan for nothing, and typical of it is the heroic couplet, like these which open the second epistle of Pope's *Essay on Man,* in which correlatives and antitheses are balanced:

> Know then thyself, presume not God to scan;
> The proper study of Mankind is Man.
> Placed on this isthmus of a middle state,
> A Being darkly wise, and rudely great:
> With too much knowledge for the Sceptic side,
> With too much weakness for the Stoic's pride,
> He hangs between: in doubt to act, or rest;
> In doubt to deem himself a God, or Beast;
> In doubt his Mind or Body to prefer:
> Born but to die, and reasoning but to err;
> Alike in ignorance, his reason such,
> Whether he thinks too little, or too much.

The heroic couplet is sometimes loosely defined as "two rimed lines of iambic pentameter," but although each line contains ten syllables, often there are four beats to a line, two on one side of the caesura and two on the other: "BORN but to DIE and REAsoning but to ERR." There is often, besides this metrical balance, rhetorical balance of correlatives and/or antitheses, as well as grammatical balance. Thus a five-beat line like the second line in Pope's *Rape of the Lock,* called a "golden line," is built like a Roman arch: the keystone in the middle is the appropriate verb "rise"—"What MIGHty CONtests RISE from TRIVial THINGS." "Mighty" and "trivial" are balanced adjectives opposed in meaning; "contests" and "things" are nouns and correlatives; and all five important words receive the accents.

There were dozens of attempts to imitate Sir John Denham's 1655 apostrophe to the Thames, to most of us now a cliché:

> O might I FLOW like THEE and MAKE thy STREAM
> My GREAT ex-AM-ple, as it IS my THEME:
> Though DEEP, yet CLEAR; though GEN-tle, yet NOT́ DÙLL;
> STRONG without RAGE; without o'er-FLOW-ing, FULL.

All we need do here is to underscore the fact that the balance of antitheses and correlatives in twos and fours, emphasized by the four-beat caesured line, is patently Empedoclean in its imitation of *concordia discors*. Dr. Johnson noticed that two pairs of adjectives applied to Denham's river are physical and two are psychological. Similarly, *Gulliver's Travels*, on its very surface, consists of two books based on a physical image and two books on a psychological one. In book 1 Gulliver is too big, and in book 2 he is too small; in book 3 he is too smart, and in book 4 he is too stupid.

Augustan wit likes the number four. There are four elements, four humors, four seasons, four directions, four secondary causes, four suits in a deck of cards. Besides the four *Georgics*, there are four books of Horace (two of epistles and two of satires), four speakers in Dryden's *Essay*, four parts to Pope's *Essay on Man*, and four books of *The Dunciad*. In the *Essay on Criticism*, Pope exhausts his illustrations of the principle of the sound echoing the sense in twos and fours. "Sound" and "sense" are correlative and antithetical. Two examples of their *concordia discors* are visual and auditory ("soft" versus "loud"), and two are visual and kinaesthetic ("slow" versus "swift").

> 'Tis not enough no harshness gives offence,
> The sound must seem an Echo to the sense:
> Soft is the strain when Zephyr gently blows,
> And the smooth stream in smoother numbers flows;
> But when loud surges lash the sounding shore,
> The hoarse, rough verse should like the torrent roar;
> When Ajax strives some rock's vast weight to throw,
> The line too labours, and the words move slow;
> Not so, when swift Camilla scours the plain,
> Flies o'er th' unbending corn, and skims along the main.
> [2. 365–73]

As Pope in successive versions improved his masterful *Rape of the Lock*, he did more than merely add the machinery of the sprites; by them he held up a pattern of *concordia* through the *discordia* they cause. From the Empedoclean four elements and the Galenian four humors, Pope gained psychological truth and mock cosmic order and disorder in patterns of twos and fours, with the attendant possibilities of both fission and fusion in that beautiful breast of Miss Arabella Fermor. Belinda is created to fulfill by her basic nature the most feminine function of charming all mankind.

But she momentarily allows the other elements of her nature to get in her way, particularly the antithesis of woman—prudery and masculinity. That the major *discordia* is between the *earth* and *air* of her nature is obvious from the fact that these two elements and their qualities are the only two given names: Ariel versus Umbriel. The *airy* Ariel gives up when he sees an *earthly* lover lurking in her mind. In parody of the Virgilian *descensus Averni* the gnome fetches from the Cave of Spleen the two middle elements, a bag of wind that acts like *fire* and a vial of tears, obviously *water*. When he throws these upon Belinda, she completely loses her balance, weeping copiously like a nymph and angrily darting fire out of her eyes like a salamander. Had she been able to quote Denham's apostrophe to the Thames on her boat ride up to Hampton Court, she would not have become such a mixed up little girl. She would be like Matthew Prior's "Jinny":

> With a just trim of Virtue her Soul was endu'd,
> Not affectedly Pious nor secretly Lewd
> She cut even between the Cocquet and the Prude.
> [Lines 49–51]

The Aristotelian ethic demands a balance between not too much of this and not too much of that.[7]

"Cooper's Hill," "Windsor Forest," and *The Essay on Man* all imitate the classical mode and shape of *concordia discors* in patterns of twos and fours. Even when there are threes as in Denham's three Virgilian views on the Thames—nearby Saint Paul's for the revival of religion, in the distance Chertsey Abbey for the destruction of religion, and, in between, the eulogized royal hill on which Windsor Castle stands—even the threes are deployed horizontally with two extremes and the center ("Where *Mars* with *Venus* dwells" (line 39) holding firm.[8] Thus the Empedoclean theory of world harmony, which consists of a careful balance between opposites, gives rise to much of Augustan wit.

Metaphysical wit, on the other hand, (and who cannot tell the difference?) arises from the other classical concept of *discordia concors* which begins with Plato and was taken over by Christian thinkers. Its seed lies in Plato's description in the *Timaeus* of how God created the universe:

> Out of the indivisible and unchangeable, and also out of that which is divisible and has to do with material bodies,

> he compounded a third and intermediate kind of essence,
> partaking of the nature of the same and of the other, and
> this compound he placed accordingly in a mean between
> the indivisible, and the divisible and material. He took the
> three elements of the same, the other, and the essence, and
> mingled them into one form, compressing by force the
> reluctant and unsociable nature of the other into the
> same.[9]

Characteristic of this pattern are the triad instead of the tetrad; the initial hierarchizing of the opposing elements; and the struggle to join the lower value into the higher to create a "new concoction," as Donne would call it.

Basic to the poetry of Donne and Herbert, which "imitates" this kind of world harmony, is an upward struggle from a lower entity to its oposing higher entity in order to achieve a third which is brand new. The "metaphysicals" did not wait for the balance of the cosmos to invade their souls; by acts of will they forced an order out of chaos even if, like Donne, they had to rape language to accomplish it. The process lies in time, not space; and it is never easy, no easier than the struggle for harmony in musical images through history that imbues Milton's "Ode on the Nativity."

Donne's "The Ecstasy" is a good example of "metaphysical wit." It is divided into three parts of twenty lines each, slightly interrupted at the end of part 1 and at the end of part 3 by an observer who, like the reader of the poem, must learn something mysterious. In the first twenty lines two souls negotiate above the lovers, who lie in a trance like sepulchral statues. In the middle twenty lines the two souls join to create a third, an abler soul that controls the defects of each one separate. The final twenty-line segment, beginning "But O alas," argues by the same serious means for the bodies to join with the new single soul, since the combining of the lower into the higher will produce a still newer third, a systasis or union greater than all that precedes. That *time* is involved in the process emerges from the fact that the three parts are past, present, and future.[10]

Again, Herbert's "Easter" clearly illustrates the poetic cast of this kind of world harmony:

> Rise, heart, thy Lord is risen; sing His praise
>   Without delays,

> Who takes thee by the hand, that thou likewise
> > With him mayst rise;
> That, as His death calcined thee to dust,
> His life may make thee gold, and, much more, just.
>
> Awake, my lute, and struggle for thy part
> > With all thy art;
> The cross taught all wood to resound His name
> > Who bore the same;
> His stretched sinews taught all strings what key
> Is best to celebrate this most high day.
>
> Consort both heart and lute, and twist a song
> > Pleasant and long;
> Or, since all music is but three parts vied
> > And multiplied,
> O, let They blessed spirit bear a part,
> And make up our defects with His sweet art.[11]

The heart and lute do not "balance"; they struggle to join together with the risen Christ, and, as Plato said, the "three" become "one."

The combining type of mind that would change Horace's separated ends of poetry, instruction *or* delight, into a single phrase like "delightful teaching" uses many words with the Latin prefix, *con-*, three times, for example, in the first four lines of Herbert's "The H. Scriptures. ii":

> Oh that I knew how all thy lights combine,
> > And the configurations of their glorie!
> > Seeing not onely how each verse doth shine,
> But all the constellations of the storie.[12]

A further effect of yoking comes from the use of words beginning with *inter-*. Every one remembers "Interassured of the mind," but John Donne also uses *interbring, interchange, intergraft, interinanimate, intertouched,* and *interwish.* Thus a characteristic metaphysical conceit is the oxymoron, like Vaughan's allusion to Dionysius the Areopagite's "dazzling darkness" that lies in God. Dr. Johnson, good Christian though he was, would say this is not an "imitation of nature"; in it "the most heterogeneous ideas are yoked by violence together."

I am not so literal a Procrustes as to force all the seventeenth century into one mold and all the eighteenth into the other. But this essay in persuasion stares at a larger canvas than some of the others, hence the broad brush. I admire the eighteenth century but love the seventeenth.

7 What Happened to Two of Herbert's Poems?

Among English poets George Herbert is noted for the accuracy of his emblematic titles, the inventiveness of his metrical and stanzaic structures, and his grasp of architectonics. That is why, when we come across something in his work that we feel is un-Herbertian, we may well ask some questions, particularly in view of the unknown circumstances surrounding the publication of his work. For years we dwelt upon Isaac Walton's lovely story of the poet, on his deathbed, giving Duncon a "little book of verses" to take to his friend Nicholas Ferrar at Little Gidding. J. Max Patrick has shown that the story is largely fabricated from Ferrar's own 1633 preface.[1] Nevertheless, there remain two manuscripts of *The Temple*: the Williams, called "W," which contains fewer poems, a different order, and many emendations, some of which are in Herbert's hand; and the Bodleian, or "B," probably made at Little Gidding, from which the first edition of 1633 appears to have been printed. Herbert's own final manuscript of *The Temple* is lost. This leaves room for speculation on what might have happened during transcription to at least two of Herbert's poems which raise peculiar problems, and another opportunity to persuade my readers that this essay may contain a solution.

Some of the material of the first part of this essay was presented orally at the University of Michigan–Dearborn Conference on George Herbert in October 1978, and published in *Essays in Literature* (Macomb, Ill.: Western Illinois University) 6 (1979): 161–66. The second argument began as "A Crux in George Herbert's *The Temple*," *English Language Notes* 7 (1970): 13–17.

One poem, "Good Friday," challenges the safe assumption that Herbert is so aware of unity that he changes the metrical scheme within a given poem only for very valid artistic reasons. The other poem, "Church-lock and key," seems to have been mistitled. Both poems, moreover, may have been given the wrong position within the structure of the whole work.

In its present state "Good Friday" manifestly consists of two parts discrete in metrical and stanzaic form, the obvious break coming at the sixth stanza:

Good Friday

[1]   O my chief good,
How shall I measure out thy bloud?
How shall I count what thee befell,
    And each grief tell?

[2]   Shall I thy woes
Number according to thy foes?
Or, since one starre show'd thy first breath,
    Shall all thy death?

[3]   Or shall each leaf
Which falls in Autumne, score a grief?
Or can not leaves, but fruit, be signe
    Of the true vine?

[4]   Then let each houre
Of my whole life one grief devoure;
That thy distresse through all may runne,
    And be my sunne.

[5]   Or rather let
My severall sinnes their sorrows get;
That as each beast his cure doth know,
    Each sinne may so.

[6]   Since bloud is fittest, Lord, to write
Thy sorrows in, and bloudie fight;
My heart hath store, writer there, where in
One box doth lie both ink and sinne:

[7]   That when sinne spies so many foes,
Thy whips, thy nails, thy wounds, thy woes,

> All come to lodge there, sinne may say,
> *No room for me*, and flie away.

[8]   Sinne being gone, oh fill the place,
       And keep possession with thy grace;
       Lest sinne take courage and return,
       And all the writings blot or burn.[2]

Either we have here a single poem, the two parts forming together a poetic unity-disunity; or we have two separate poems of
different titles and ordering, their conjunction and shift in position resulting from some other hand than that of the poet. It might
be argued by one taking the first stance that Herbert changed his
form at stanza 6 in order to oppose the emphases upon Christ in
part 1 and upon the sinner in part 2; or that in part 1 the poet asks
how he can "measure" or "count" or "tell" the sufferings of
Christ, and in the second part answers the question in view of his
"several" sins (stanza 5). And yet, as we shall see by comparing
this with other "double" poems by Herbert, the shift in form has
no such immediately apprehended artistic function; and the image
in the second part—of blood, ink, and writing—appears un-
justified. It is not his mere writing of poetry that Herbert is prepared to give; in stanza four it is his whole life that he is willing to
sacrifice.

In the W manuscript the present "Good Friday" is two separate
poems, the first five stanzas named "Good Friday," and the last
three, "The Passion," a poem by itself, placed earlier in the sequence immediately after "The Reprisall" (p. 36). I shall argue that
"Good Friday" become once more two separate poems (as in the
W manuscript); that its present second part be once more entitled
"The Passion" (meaning of course the poet's passion in imitation
of Christ); and that it be restored to its original position, before,
not after, the first part of the present "Good Friday." My hypothesis that some one, without the authorization of the poet, changed
titles and shifted positions of poems in the initial cycle of *The
Temple* must (1) satisfy a set of historical and textual facts, and (2)
coincide with literary traits perceivable within the Holy Week
cycle, of which "Good Friday" is a part, and within the whole of
The Temple.

In the B-manuscript the present second part of "Good Friday"
appears on a separate page but has no title. If an amanuensis or
Nicholas Ferrar made the changes in position and collocation, we

can only conjecture a motive. So near the beginning of a book, he may have been disturbed by the appearance of two poems bearing the same title, for within the brief Holy Week cycle which opens the work there were two poems called "The Thanksgiving," two poems called "The Passion," and two poems called "H. Baptisme." He may have changed one title in each of the first two pairs, and by the time he came to the baptism poems realized that this doubling was a deliberate device of Herbert's. The several later sets of repeated titles in *The Temple* he did not attempt to "improve."

The assumption that unauthorized changes were made from W to B/1633 at the beginning of *The Temple*, despite Ferrar's denial in "The Printer to the Reader," is strengthened by what actually happened to the two introductory quatrains. The W manuscript gives to the first quatrain a page to itself with the title "Perirranterium," meaning the vessel for sprinkling holy water during the preparation for priesthood. The second quatrain in W is likewise alone, on the opposite page, with the title "Superliminare," But B and 1633 have both quatrains on a single page (Hutchinson, p. 25) with the inappropriate title "Superliminaire." Hutchinson's commentary makes plain the evidence of nonauthorial tampering:

> [The two quatrains] stand midway between *The Church-Porch* and *The Church*, and belong to neither. They do not constitute a single poem: the first quatrain invites the reader of *The Church-Porch* (*the former precepts,* line 1) to enter *The Church*: the second, to which alone, and more appropriately, the title *Superliminare* is given in *W*, is conceived as inscribed on the lintel . . . and warns off *Profanenesse* from going farther. [P. 484]

The hypothetical solution to the problem of "Good Friday" becomes more credible as we join to these textual and historical facts the literary traits perceivable in the cycle of Holy Week. As Herbert's year began on 25 March, he begins his book with the season when the church celebrates the sacrifice of Christ "for us men and for our salvation." In the front of the first group of poems, as well as of the book, *"The Altar"* becomes the symbol of sacrifice. Then follows the highly dramatic monologue of Christ called "The Sacrifice," and the cycle proceeds through the "Passion" (suffering), the Death on the cross, and the Resurrection. It ends with the sacrament that flowed from the water and blood issuing from the dead Christ's pierced side, Baptism (cf. "The Sacrifice," lines 245–7, and the first "H. Baptisme," lines 5–6).

The holy week between Palm Sunday and Easter is signified by Christ's calling himself "the meek / And readie Paschall Lambe of this great week" ("The Sacrifice," lines 58–59); and in "The Sinner" Herbert wants to make his soul "even with the week" (p. 38, line 3). The historical events of his last week on earth narrated by Christ (pp. 26–34) are so carefully ordered that "The Sacrifice" becomes crucial to the ordering of poems that follow it in the Easter cycle. In chronicling the events of the week in that poem, Herbert follows very strictly the biblical chronology, as can be shown by listing the following key phrases and incidents in "The Sacrifice" with their parallel sequence in Mark, chapters 14 and 15, the Gospel lessons appointed to be read on the Monday and Tuesday before Easter. Not once does Herbert's chronology deviate from the narrative order or verses in Mark:

"The Sacrifice" (line)	Incident	Mark (chap.: verse)
13	Judas Iscariot	14:10
17	thirty pence	14:11
23	let this cup pass	14:36
28	disciples sleep	14:37
37	clubs, staves	14:48
49	disciples flee	14:50
53	from one ruler to another	14:53
65	temple, three days	14:58
73	Pontius Pilate	15:1
97	"Crucify him!"	15:13
113	Barrabus	15:15
125	"they scourge me"	15:15
161	crown of thorns	15:17
173	"Hail king!"	15:18
190	"mine own clothes"	15:20
199	Simon bears the cross	15:21
213	"My God, why leav'st thou me?"	15:34
249	Christ dies	15:37

Adhering to the barest outline of Christ's suffering and death, Herbert concentrates on the "grief" suffered by Christ at the cruel mockery of hailing as "king" him who is the True King. Though we say, "He *suffered* death upon the cross," the suffering is usually considered to have preceded "the ninth hour"; at the moment of death, the "Passion" came to an end. And yet the second part of "Good Friday" lists "thy sorrows," "bloudie fight," "thy whips, thy nails, thy wounds, thy woes" to denote Herbert's willingness to take unto himself the "Passion" (original title) of Christ. His *death*, on the other hand, is not something to imitate but to be thankful for. (Cf. "The Dawning," p. 112).

In this initial cycle, the ordering of poems in W and B/1633 is fairly similar despite the necessity to accommodate two new poems, "The Agonie" and "The Sepulchre." The "Thanksgiving" poems, contiguous in W, are kept contiguous in B/1633. The two "Passion" poems of W are also kept contiguous but are moved to a later spot in the series, that is, after "Good Friday" instead of before. In its original position, the second "Passion" (renamed "Redemption," p. 40), in the last line of which Christ dies, was a beautifully understated parable to introduce "Good Friday," the second stanza of which predicates Christ's death. In B/1633 both parts of "Good Friday" follow "The Sinner," but I believe that only the second part (originally the first "Passion") should, because of the imagistic connection between the two poems. "The Sinner" ends with with "Remember that thou once didst *write* in stone," and the first "Passion" begins, "Since blood is fittest, Lord, to *write* / Thy sorrows in" (my italics). The New Law taking the place of the Old (Mosaic) Law became clear with the suffering and death of Christ. On the whole, the Easter cycle of poems in W is historically and theologically better arranged than in B/1633.

Reading the present "Good Friday" within the larger context of the whole of Herbert's poetry, we are surprised by the sudden change in metric form between the two parts. A flair for the architectonic is a byword with all readers of Herbert, for his two favorite arts besides poetry were evidently music and architecture. He not only built his poems but rebuilt his churches at Leighton, Bromswold, and Bemerton. In construction, all must be of a piece. "Vanitie ii", (p. 111), for example, contains three heroic couplets at the beginning and a single heroic couplet at the end, but the ten lines between, of an entirely different cast, function as a new little "heavenly" poem to warn the "poore silly soul" of the poet against the "earthly" love poems he had contemplated "writing for sweet." The final lines, again a heroic couplet, ring out the moral.

Such artistic decorum can be specially tested in those few poems in *The Temple* that consist patently of two separate parts which yet become one poem despite the difference in rhyme, meter, or line length. Consider "Easter" within the cycle we are talking about (pp. 41–42). In W it was two separate poems, and only Herbert himself could have joined the present second part to the first as the promised "song" (line 13) of praise on Easter Day. Similarly, "An Offering" (pp. 147–48) makes its second part the actual offering described in the first part: "Then bring thy gift, and let thy hymn be this," Herbert says, and the "hymn" so offered should consist of a different form. A third example of a double poem whose two parts architectonically cohere despite a shift in poetic form is "Christmas" (pp. 80–81). Only the first part of this poem appears in W, but Herbert (for no amanuensis could have done it) added a second part, in different rhyme, to become the song sung by the shepherds and by the poet to celebrate this day—like the proem and the hymn in Milton's "On the Morning of Christ's Nativity." Finally, "The Church-floore" (pp. 66–67) is a double poem whose second part is set in different meter and rhyme, as sin, like dust, spoils the four-square neatness of the carefully constructed stone floor of the first part of the poem. Thus Herbert's double poems, like the literary device of "the play within the play," sustain a nexus between the inner and outer plots. Herbert would no more inexplicably change his meter and rhyme scheme within a single poem than he would countenance a disordered service, a surprise ending to a piece of music, or three ungainly cornices stuck onto the wing of a house. He outlawed one who "liking not the fashion, / Began to make Balcones, Terraces, / Till she had weakned all by alteration" ("The World," p. 84). This makes the questionable coherence in "Good Friday" all the more glaring.

Since my hypothetical solution for the problem of "Good Friday," then, does not violate the known historical facts and is consonant with the observed literary traits of Herbert's work, I suggest that the second part of "Good Friday" be a separate poem as it once was, entitled "The Passion" and placed with "Redemption" before "Good Friday," its original position.

The following order of poems in the Easter cycle makes greater poetic and religious sense: the first seven poems as printed in Hutchinson—(1) the second quatrain of "Superliminare," (2) "The Altar," (3) "The Sacrifice," (4) "The Thanksgiving," (5) "The Reprisall," (6) "The Agonie," (7) "The Sinner." Then I suggest that the rest of the poems in the cycle be read seriatim as follows: (8)

the second part of "Good Friday," entitled "The Passion," (9) "Redemption," (10) the first part of "Good Friday," (11) "Sepulchre," (12) "Easter," (13) "Easter-wings," (14, 15) the two "Baptisme" poems.

Thus Herbert opens his "Church" with Holy Week, a time among all Anglicans for baptism, confirmation, and reaffirmation, and, with the oncoming of spring, the general renewal of Christian faith. As a foundation to his "building" there must be nothing awry.

The problem with the other poem is not quite so complex.[3]

> *Church-lock and key*
> I know it is my sinne, which locks thine eares,
>   And bindes thy hands,
> Out-crying my requests, drowning my tears;
> Or else the chilnesse of my faint demands.
>
> But as cold hands are angrie with the fire,
>   And mend it still;
> So I do lay the want of my desire,
> Not on my sinnes, or coldnesse, but thy will.
>
> Yet heare, O God, onely for his blouds sake
>   Which pleads for me:
> For though sinnes plead too, yet like stones they make
> His blouds sweet current much more loud to be.
>
>   [Hutchinson, p. 66]

I think it is a beautiful poem, but why "Church-lock and key" and what has this poem to do with such ecclesiastical adjuncts as "Church-monuments" and "The Church-floor" among which it appears? There are "keys" to God's kingdom, but what is the "church-lock"? In "The Glimpse" (p. 154), we have " . . . the droppings of the stock / May oft break forth, and never break the lock." In "Confession" (p. 126), Herbert wrote "No smith can make such locks but they have keyes"; and "Longing" (p. 149) contains the line, "Is all lockt? hath a sinners plea / No key?" In present-day punctuation, instead of "Church-lock and key," the title might become "Church Lock-and-key" to intend that a lock and key go together like mortise-and-tenon. But the poem that now follows the title seems to concern private prayer rather than the liturgical prayer of the *church*. What is more, the most striking image, that of Christ's blood rushing in a torrent against the stones of the sinner's stony heart to make a sound that catches the ear of God, is hardly controlled by either a *lock* or a *key*.

Nevertheless the eighteenth-century George Ryley, whose piety outran his critical insight, took the metaphor very literally in "Mr. Herberts Temple & Church Militant Explained and Improved by A Discourse upon Each Poem Critical & Practical": "The Use of a Lock & Key, are to Secure anyplace from being entered, without the will of the proprietor; or to give admittance to whom he will. In the church God himself is the proprietor, and he has Committed to his Stewards the Use of the Lock & Keyes, to exclude the Ex-communicates, and admit the professor to pay Homage to him. Now every one that is in the outer court is not able to pierce within the pale."[3] It is scarcely necessary to point out how ill this interpretation consorts with the spirit of the rector of Bemerton.

The W version of the poem now under discussion is by comparison very poor, though its title may be more appropriate:

Prayer
I know it is my sinne, which stops thine eares,
            And bindes thy hand,
Out-crying my requests, drowning my tears;
Or else the chilnesse of my faint demands.

If either Innocence or ffervencie
            did play their part
Armies of blessings would contend & vye
Wch of them soonest should attaine my hart.

Yet as cold hands are angrie with the fire
            Mending it still;
So I do lay the want of my desire,
Not on my coldnesse, but thy will.

O make mee wholy guiltles, or at least
            Guiltles so farr;
That zele and pureness circling my request
May guard it safe beyond ye highest starr.[4]

We must assume that Herbert himself made the improvements from W to B. A useless second stanza is expunged, inorganic images (like the final one on astronomy) are omitted, and the petitioner's questionable desire to be "guiltless" is now directed to his dependence upon God's grace. The first revision from W to B occurs in the very first line: the word "stops" becomes "locks," which seems to be the only justification for changing the title from "Prayer" to "Church-lock and key." "Stops" is more appropriate to the stones-water image with which the poem closes.

Even more baffling than the new title is the different position of this poem in the two manuscripts. As we have just seen, the initial cycle in B/1633, the Easter cycle, ends with the two "Baptisme" poems. In W there followed two poems on "Love" and a poem then called "The H. Communion." This poem is entirely omitted from B/1633, and substituted for it is a new poem, also "The H. Communion" (Hutchinson, p. 52), which consists of two quite separate parts with a four-line space separating them (B ms., fol. 34). This is the only occurrence of such a phenomenon in the entire B manuscript, and Hutchinson notes that "it may have been intended to insert a title in this space." The first part of the poem describes the elements of the Eucharist as being sufficient to prompt God's grace. And the second part, after the blank, is the W poem originally called "Prayer—Give me my captive soul." Query: Was this space left blank for the possible insertion of the title "Church-lock and key"?

Yes, if the images of the first part of the new "H. Communion" are any clue. Beginning "Not in rich furniture, or fine aray," the poem asserts that the bread and wine "spread their forces into every part" but cannot "get over to my soul, / *Leaping the wall* that parts / Our souls and fleshy hearts" (my italics). Rather than vainly trying to leap over the wall, it is better to unlock the gate, if one has the key. Hence (stanza 4):

> Onely thy grace, which with these elements come,
> > Knoweth the ready way
> > And *hath the privie key*,
> > *Op'ning* the souls most subtile *roomes*;
> While those to spirits refin'd, at *doore* attend
> > Dispatches from their friend.

[My italics]

Inside the locked enclosure of our hearts, once the door is opened by the church sacrament and God's grace, stands God himself ready to hand us his message.

The blank four-line space that immediately follows this might well be filled with the title "Church-lock and key," moreover, because the poem that the space introduces is actually a petition to be used at the close of the church's central sacrament and the communicant's voluntary participation in it:

> Give me my captive soul, or take
> My bodie thither....

> For sure when Adam did not know
> To sinne, or sinne to smother;
> He might to heav'n from Paradise go
> *As from one room t'another.*

> Thou hast *restor'd* us to this ease
> By *this* thy heav'nly bloud
> Which I can go to, when I please,
> And leave th'earth to their food.

The first Adam had the key and lost it. His descendants were "locked" out until the second Adam, Christ, "restored" the key in the church sacrament that commemorates his sacrifice, the church founded by Saint Peter, to whom Christ gave the "keys" (Matt. 16:19).

Whatever happened from W to B, the present "Church-lock and key" was caught up in it. The printer of 1633 did his best to cement the new arrangement, for he removed the anagram on "Mary" and "Army" from its position in B between "Church-musique" and the poem we are talking about—"the only difference in the order of poems in B from that adopted in 1633" (Hutchinson, p. 77). The new title and the new ordering of our poem, then, indeed invite the kind of questions we ask, even though the answers can only be conjectural. Surely, the two parts of the present "H. Communion" no more fit together than do the two parts of the present "Good Friday."

I strongly suspect that the amanuensis of B failed to understand the title "Church-lock and key" for the separate poem which is now the second part of "The H. Communion," and being in doubt, left the space for it. Then he may have placed the leftover title before a poem called "Prayer" because there were already two poems called "Prayer" and this poem had in its first line the word "locks." Finally, misled by his own title he may have placed this poem among other poems that take their emblems from various accoutrements of church architecture, such as floors, windows, etc.

On the basis of history, manuscript evidence, and literary

analysis, then, I suggest that the poem now so awkwardly entitled "Church-lock and key" be called what Herbert once called it, "Prayer," and that it be read not with "monuments" and "windows" but in the position where Herbert once placed it, next to the masterful sonnet "Prayer the church's banquet . . . something understood."[5]

The final test of my two hypotheses lies in the experience of the reader who knows the history of *The Temple* and is alive to Herbert's religious and poetic sensibility. There can be no proof, only persuasion.[6]

8   Who "Confuted" John Milton in 1642?

The controversy between Bishop Joseph Hall and Milton has been examined several times but almost invariably from the point of view of the more famous contestant. The purpose of this essay in persuasion is to read the adversary who engendered Milton's angriest piece of prose as carefully as we have been reading Milton, and thereby to lend support to W. R. Parker's early suggestion that the "Confuter" was not Bishop Hall but the Reverend Robert Dunkin, a loyal and little known vicar in Hall's own diocese.

First, a brief resumé of the events that led up to the confrontation. At Archbishop Laud's behest, Bishop Hall of Exeter published, in February 1640, *Episcopacie by Divine Right,* and in January 1641, continued the official plea for Anglicanism in *An Humble Remonstrance,* this time aided by his scholarly friend James Ussher, archbishop of Armagh. Challenged by the five Smectymnuuans in March 1641, Hall had to publish *A Defence of the Humble Remonstrance* (April 1641). After a *Vindication* by Smectymnuus and another *Short Answer* from Hall, John Milton came to the aid of his five Puritan friends: first against Archbishop Ussher, and then, in *Animadversions upon the Remonstrant's Defence against Smectymnuus* (winter 1642) against the bishop of Exeter. This personal attack on Hall brought forth in his defence *A Modest Confutation of the Animadversions upon the Remonstrant against Smectymnuus* (winter 1642), which, the following April, drew from

Part of this material appears as chapter 11 of my book on Bishop Hall (Cambridge: D. S. Brewer, 1979). Reprinted by permission.

Milton the *Apology against a Pamphlet call'd A Modest Confutation of the Animadversions upon the Remonstrant against Smectymnuus.*

Since the last three items, all anonymous, present us with the drama of two unknown pamphleteers leaping at each other in the dark, each speaking for more important and publicly known persons, I shall call the author we now know as John Milton the "Animadverter" or the "Apologist" and the unidentified person who spoke for Bishop Hall the "Confutant."[1] Whoever he was, he did not know that he was arguing against Milton. "I have no further notice of [the Animadverter]," he writes, "than he hath been pleased ... to give of himself, and therefore, as our industrious Criticks for want of clearer evidence concerning the life and manners of revived Authours, must fetch his character from scattered passages in his own writings" (p. A 3 r).

The worst things the Confutant says about the defamer of his friend Bishop Hall come in the short "To the Reader: "There is thrust forth upon the Stage ... a scurrilous Mime, a personated, and (as himself thinks) a grim, lowring, bitter fool." Having been "vomited out" from the university, this "mime" is now living in a "suburbe sinke about London, which, since his comming up, hath groaned under two ills, Him, and the Plague." If you want to find him after dinner, the Confutant adds, search in the theaters, bordelli, etc. This is certainly close to libel, but the key to it is the playhouse image, which is not the Confutant's but comes from the *Animadversions.* The Animadverter had announced in his Preface that he is purposely adopting a role of "grim laughter"; and the Confutant (p. 34) picks up further references to that theatrical role in the Animadverter's use of "Modena masks," "vizards," etc. (I, p. 711).

The Confutant argues that the Animadverter's language ("scurrility") does not become religious controversy and that the incessant name-calling amounts to "libel." On the very first page he quotes a long list of such vituperations as "spiritual fornication," "cogging of dice into Heaven," "gleeking and Bacchanalia," etc., and concludes: "Such language you should hear from the mouths of canting beggars, at an heathen altar; much less was it looked for in a treatise of controversial Theologie, as yours might have been thought, had you not thus prevented it" (p. 2).

Even so, when he quotes his adversary's language, he omits its saltier aspects. For example, here for comparison are three of the

Animadverter's original phrases with the Confutant's quotations of them (p. A. 3v): (1) Animadverter—"a gallopping Nun, Proffering herself, but wee heare of none that bids money for her" (p. 680); Confutant—"like an English gallopping Nun": (2) Animadverter—"vainglorious . . . like the desire of *Tamar*, who to raise seed to her Husband sate in the common road drest like a Courtesan, and he that came to her committed incest with her" (p. 688); Confutant—"A Pharisaicall and vainglorious project"; (3) Animadverter—"than a wife affecting whorish attire kindles a disturbance in the eye of her discerning husband" (p. 687); Confutant—"than a wife affecting whorish attire." The whore-of-Babylon conceit for Rome was a commonplace; but although he is as anti-Roman (being English) as any Anglican or Presbyterian, the Confutant sedulously expurgates the Animadverter's more sexual treatments of the metaphor. "Christian," he asks in possible mock innocence, "dost thou like these passages, or doth thy heart rise against such unseemly beastlinesse?"

As the Confutant for the most part avoids scurrilous language, so in defending Hall against libel he steers fairly clear of the sin he condemns. Like the shocking vocabulary he quotes, most of what seems to be personal opprobrium consists of phrases taken from the *Animadversions* and turned back upon their author. For example, the Apologist is appalled (p. 883) at the Confutant's implying that he, the Apologist, had spent his youth in "loytering, bezzelling, and harlotting" (*Modest Confutation*, p. 3 r); but it was the Animadverter who had first said that *all prelates* "spend their youth in loitering, bezzling, and harlotting" (p. 677). Again, the Confutant's charge, "You can be as bold with a Prelate, as familiar with your Laundresse" (p. 9), struck the Apologist as such calumny as to call for passionate protestations of his own chastity; whereas the Confutant is merely alluding to the Animadverter's assertion that a bishop's "surplesse" and the priest of Isis's "lawne sleeves" "may for holinesse lie together in the suds" (p. 729). No one accused the Apologist of fornicating with his washerwoman.

Throughout, the Confutant makes it clear that what some Miltonists have taken to be personal vilification comes originally from the author of the *Animadversions*. He accuses the Animadverter of atheism and sedition against King and Parliament on the grounds of the language used; charging him with handling such matters "in such a wretched, loathsome manner" as to jeer at "religion, and God, and all" (p. 6). Quotations of that languge carry his point. For example, "If [Bishop Hall] write controversies, then he is a Swashbuckler against the Pope; . . . If he preaches, then he sermonizes and dawbes with untempered mortar; If at Court, he is crowding for preferment, or accusing the people to the King; If at home, he is a belly-God, &c. O the love, and charity, and reverence of these times, to so holy, so deserving a Bishop" (p. 20). The *Modest Confutation* brims over with language like this, but it is the Animadverter's language. "Neither in this point," the Confutant says in another context, "would I ever have condemned ye, had I not heard it from your own mouths" (p. 21). He is shocked by the lack of Christian charity that lies behind the Animadverter's attack on Hall's person, especially (p. 5) in view of the Animadverter's self-expressed determination to write "without all private and personal spleene" (p. 663); nevertheless, the Confutant concludes, "it is the greatest matter in your book."[2]

Having spent three-quarters of the *Confutation* on his adversary's scurrilous and libelous language, the anonymous author comes to the argument, a proportion he takes to be approximately that of tantrum to reason in the *Animadversions*. "The scraps and offall that remain of your Libell, concern Liturgie and Episcopacie: both of which you have handled, as you esteem of them, unworthily and basely," he says (p. 21). By "scraps" he means the method of quoting disconnected passages from Hall out of context and answering them; and by "offal" he means the disgust, obvious to every reader, that Hall's detractor evinces at the mere mention of *The Book of Common Prayer* and Anglican ecclesiastical polity. After defending his friend, the Confutant defends his church on the usual Anglican grounds. He is practical, moderate, and eloquent, reflecting the temper of Hooker, whom (unlike Hall) he often appeals to. At the end he becomes soberly prophetic: "You say that set forms of Prayers are quenching to the Spirit; whether it be so or no, I am sure your Extemporall will set such a fire on your Spirits, that they will need quenching, or the whole Kingdome will burn with them. Weigh these circumstances, and you will see that there is an expediency of set forms in a nationall Church" (p. 30).

The Apologist had no more notice of the author of *A Modest Confutation* (as the Confutant said of the Animadverter) "than he hath been pleased... to give of himself." As evidence of authorship he cites Bishop Hall's three anti-Smectymnuuan pamphlets (*Apology*, p. 876). Elsewhere, however, he wonders whether the author of the *Remonstrance* (Bishop Hall) and of the *Modest Confutation* "be not one person, or as I am told, Father and Son" (p. 897). Throughout the *Apology* he seems to waver between the aging bishop and a young collegiate whom he addresses as "thou lozell Bachelour of Art" (p. 920).

Since the Confutant was clever enough to flush the Apologist out into the open, we might as well call the Apologist John Milton. Milton assumed from three passages in *A Modest Confutation* that there was a young collaborator. When he justified his own "grim laughter" as part of the mask of the *Animadversions* by saying that "grave Authoures" recommend it as a pedagogical device (1: 663–64), the Confutant responds: "I care not to know what your reading hath been: mine own is confest small" (p. 2). He quotes one "grave author," Sir Francis Bacon, against turning religious controversy into comedy or satire; that is, a single author ("small reading") is pitted against Milton's failure to mention any. Again, the Confutant confesses that he is not very well read in the history of church councils: "I conjectured your ignorance in that kind of learning to be ... as much and great as mine" (p. 34). This could be a slur on the Puritan's usual rejection of patristics, and a modest disclaimer of his own knowledge. Finally, to Milton's suggestion (p. 718) that all financial support by church and nobility of students at Oxford and Cambridge be stopped, the Confutant answers: "It is one of those young Scholars that asks your Eldership" (p. 36). This could mean that the Confutant at one time had been such a scholar, and "Your Eldership" sounds like a pun on the possible antiquity of the Smectymnuuans and an office in the Presbyterian church. These are the only possible hints of the Confutant's own age.

Now the Confutant could not be Bishop Hall. He was in the Tower from 30 December 1641 to 5 May 1642 and had other things on his mind, such as Parliament, a five-thousand-pound fine, winding up his affairs in Exeter, and readying himself for his new duties in Norwich. Besides, he spent a good part of the five months in prison writing his autobiography. Moreover, Bishop Hall had deplored the personal level on which the Smectymnuuans had chosen to wage this controversy. "I talk of 'false and frivolous exceptions,'" Hall wrote, "they say, I call them false and frivolous men. I talk of 'vain cavils'; they charge me to say that they are vain cavillers."[3] Only once in his career as polemicist had Hall used *ad hominem* argument, this to a "detested Jesuit."[4] Disgusted, he withdrew from the Smectymnuuan controversy. Finally, *A Modest Confutation* is so filled with praise of Bishop Hall that Hall could not have written it, nor, I believe, authorized it.

If the author or collaborator was a young man, as Milton temporarily suspected, could he have been one of Hall's sons? Professor Taft summarizes the possibilities in a brief note: "Masson (2:393–398) says the Confutant was Robert Hall, two years ahead of Milton at Cambridge. Parker (pp. 266–69) questions Masson's identification. Jochums, p. 3, argues for another son, Edward Hall" (Yale *Milton*, 1:863, n. 4). There is no evidence for either one, not even an argument.

As a matter of fact, the Confutant shows himself to be no mere "college matriculant" but mature in the range of his reading. He alludes to and quotes Persius, Martial, Juvenal, Aristotle's *Ethics* as well as the *Politics*, Macrobius, Pliny, Horace's *Ars Poetica*, Suetonius, Lactantius, Plautus. That he is literary-minded and au courant with the times he lived in is shown by the large number of moderns he quotes, ranging from Chaucer to his own contemporaries. Several times he quotes Hooker, Bacon, and Sandys. He had read Donne's *Pseudo-Martyr*, Sidney's *Defence of Poesy*, Ben Jonson's *Catiline*, du Moulin, Meric Casaubon, Sir David Lindsey, Hugo Grotius, du Jon ("Junius"), Machiavelli, and a host of others.

He writes a crisp, witty style, sprinkled with proverbial lore and some very beautiful images. He talks of "bowmen quick in the delivery of their arrows [but] wide of the mark" (p. 8). To him church organs, anthems, copes, and all the accoutrements of Anglican worship are only aids to devotion, not any part of the Christian creed: "That soul that can soar aloft upon the strength of his own wings, or hath its flagging Pinions completely ymped with feathers from the *Dove*, the spirit of God, shall little need such advantages as are these things . . .; only take you heed you do not, *Icarus*-like, over-dare, and give all the Christian world else leave to acknowledge and remedy as they may, their almost irremediable weaknesses" (p. 32). He seems to have learned something about writing English prose from Joseph Hall, whose *Occasional Medita-*

tions (twice alluded to) in praise of God for his creatures possibly inspired a passage like this: "He can raise Manna into our mouths, as well as dew upon the earth. Shall we be angry, because we have our Corn at the second hand? he could have sent us into the world with our cloathes on; is it not as well that he set the worm to the wheel to spin it for us" (p. 39, misnumbered 38)?

These must have been among the reasons for Milton himself to give up on "the [young] lozell Bachelour of Art." In the *Second Defence* (1654) he summarized his quarrel of a dozen years before with "two Bishops of particularly high repute": "I replied to one of the bishops [this is Ussher] in two books, *Of Prelatical Episcopacy* and *The Reason of Church-Government*, while to the other bishop [Hall] I made reply in *Animadversions* and later in an *Apology*" (Yale *Milton*, 4 pt. 1:622–23).

A few further hints of the life and character of the Modest Confutant emerge from scattered passages in his brief. We can assume he is a Royalist and an Anglican, very probably in orders. He tells us he has been abroad: "I have seen beyond the sea what the Jesuites of our own nation have carped at Master *Fox* for his History" (p. 7). He is intimate with Bishop Hall and with his writings. Above all, like the Bishop whom he defends he is large-minded and cannot make the Christian gate any narrower than Christ himself made it for those who do not in all points believe and worship as he does (p. 18). Such is the anonymous author who was responsible for Milton's combining in the *Apology* bitter, petty, sarcastic wrangling with noble passages of self-revelation. Who was he?

The person who seems best to fit the qualifications is the Reverend Robert Dunkin of Cornwall, a man whose connection with Milton was first suggested by J. Milton French, and more accurately tied to the early 1640s by William Riley Parker, though with little supporting evidence.

In John Walker's *Sufferings of the Clergy* (London, 1714) appears under Bishop Hall's own diocese, consisting of Devon and Cornwall, this entry: "DUNKIN, Robert, A. M. *St. Stephens* in Cornwell. He was one of the most learned of all *Cornish* clergy, lived to be Restored, and Preached the first *Assize-Sermon* at *Launceton* after his Majesty's Return. He published some things against Milton" (pt. 2, p. 229). John Walker (1674–1747) was himself born in Exeter, his father becoming the mayor of the city; he

was rector of Upton Pyne church in Devonshire, and lies buried in
Exeter cathedral. According to the *DNB:* "Walker collected par-
ticulars by help of query sheets, circulated in various dioceses;
those for Exeter (very minute) and Canterbury are printed by
[Edmund] Calamy (Church and Dissenters Compar'd, 1719, pp. 4,
10)." It is apparent that Walker made more compendious and more
astute enquiries in his own diocese (which had been that of
Bishop Hall, born exactly one hundred years before Walker) than
for any other diocese.

A. G. Matthews in *Walker Revised* (Oxford, 1948) identifies
Dunkin's university, Oxford, and a second parish, "vicar of St.
Michael Caerhays, 1667" (a mistake for 1637). Matthews had evi-
dently checked Foster's *Oxford Alumni,* but chose to omit the name
of Dunkin's college. Foster's complete entry is: "Dunkin, Robert,
of Cornwall, pleb. Wadham Coll., matric. 19 May, 1615, aged 16;
B.A. 4 Feb., 1618–19, M.A. 25 June, 1621, Vicar of Caerhayes,
Cornwall, 1637" (*Alumni Oxonienses* [1891], 1:433).

J. Milton French, in *Life Records of Milton* (1949–53), discusses
Robert Dunkin in relation to Phillips's reference to "some little
scribing quack in London," dating the reference to events of 1660
to 1674 (4:293–94; 5:56, 455). But Parker points out (*Biography*
[1968], 2:1145) that there Phillips is plainly talking of events in
1673, too late for Dunkin, who was born in 1599. If, as Walker
said, Dunkin had anything to do with Milton, Parker is inclined
to set his attack earlier, in the 1640s. Parker, therefore, comes
closer to my hypothesis than any one else: "Dunkin may have
been the anonymous author of the 1642 *Modest Confutation* or the
1644 *Answer to . . . The Doctrine and Discipline of Divorce*" (2:1081).

For the following reasons, then, I believe that Robert Dunkin
was the "Modest Confutant":

1. The hypothesis explains Walker's 1714 notation: "He wrote
   some things against Milton."

2. As for his age, which confused Milton, Dunkin was young
   enough to look upon Bishop Hall with fillial reverence and yet
   old enough to enter a controversy of considerable significance.
   If Dunkin matriculated at Wadham College, Oxford, in 1615 at
   the age of sixteen (Foster), he was forty-three years old in 1642.
   Milton was thirty-three and relatively unknown.

3. His is a mature piece of writing, fulfilling Walker's estimate of Dunkin as "one of the most learned of all Cornish clergy."

4. *A Modest Confutation* is not as "scurrilous" and "libelous" as it has been made out to be by Miltonists, who, naturally, have not been very kind to Bishop Hall. The genuine shock at Milton's language befits a clergyman, and he is obviously a Church of England clergyman.

5. The Confutant knows, admires, and loves Bishop Hall. Dunkin had been serving, probably for fifteen years, in one of Bishop Hall's four archdeaneries, that of Cornwall. He has given us some rare and eloquent character sketches of the bishop, aged sixty-seven, at a climactic moment in his life. The Confutant makes the earliest references to Hall's beautiful *Occasional Meditations* (1631, 1633).

6. The absence of Calvinistic and Ramistic principles, on the one hand, and the presence, on the other, of strong royalist sympathies, including a ringing plea for Charles I, point toward the author's having been trained at Oxford rather than at Cambridge. Dunkin was an Oxford man and is remembered as having given "the first Assize-Sermon at Launceton after His Majesty's return."[5] We need to know much more about the Reverend Robert Dunkin.

Bishop Hall never mentions Milton's name, though in his book on casuistry in 1643 he joins the chorus in condemning the divorce pamphlets (*Works*, 7:371). And though in 1629 he had chided his friend and fellow clergyman Hugh Cholmley for attempting to defend him in print against Henry Burton (*Works*, 8:756), he remains silent on the ally who took up the cudgels for him against an opponent of greater stature.

Hall was facing more serious issues. After only eleven months as effective Bishop of Norwich, he was ejected by the Act of Sequestration and saw his beautiful Norwich cathedral vandalized and desecrated by Parliamentary soldiers.

9   Browne's Masterpiece, *Vulgar Errors*

Sir Thomas Browne suffers, like Jeremy Taylor, from having written some of the most beautiful prose in our language. Style cannot be studied by itself, for if it is not idea it is nothing. *Religio Medici* is great in both ideas and style, but it is a desultory work of Browne's young manhood. *Hydriotaphia* is also great, and even greater with its companion piece *The Garden of Cyrus*. Browne's masterpiece, the work he spent the greatest amount of energy and time on and by means of which he made his English and Continental reputation, is *Pseudodoxia Epidemica; or, Enquiries into Very Many Received Tenets and Commonly Presumed Truths, which Examined Prove but Vulgar and Common Errors.*[1] We have come to call it simply *Vulgar Errors*. Browne planned the work early and kept it by him late, expanding each of the six editions between 1646 and 1672, the last one with a new honor to his name—Thomas Browne, M.D., KNIGHT. If it is read at all today, it is read for the quaint and pathetic zeal with which Browne demolishes long-forgotten "popular errors."

My purpose here is a double one: to grasp as surely as I can the meaning of the work; and in the process to illustrate a method of analytical reading appropriate to that large part of literature that lies outside of what we call "imaginative," literature that through

The argument of this essay is adapted from my book on Browne (1962). A different version, written for my Japanese colleagues, many of whom are charter members of the Milton Center of Japan (Doshisha University, Kyoto), appeared in *Studies Presented to Professor Naozo Ueno* (Kyoto: Doshisha University, 1963).

dialectic and rhetoric (ancient arts of language) appeals more to the reason than to the emotions.

From the very title Browne's purpose is clear. *Pseudo-* means "false"; *doxia*, "opinions." *Epidemica* is a medical metaphor: *epi-*, something laid on, that is, a disease produced by special causes not generally and continually present in the infected locality. Browne sets himself to cure the "epidemic" of error as a doctor would, first by investigating the cause of the disease, and then by prescribing the cure. The long first book is devoted to the causes, and in the following six books he treats hundreds of cases of error to the "determinators of truth."

In book 1 Browne lays down three main causes for the epidemic. The eleven chapters of book 1 arrange themselves like this:
1. The first cause of error: the common infirmity of human nature (chap. 1): a further illustration of the same (chap. 2).
2. The second cause of error: the erroneous disposition of the people:
   A. Misapprehension among common people (chap. 3),
   B. False logic among both common and educated people (chap. 4).
3. The third cause of error: easy belief (credulity) and laziness (supinity) (chap. 5):
   A. Shown in an obstinate adherence to antiquity (chap. 6),
   B. Shown in an obstinate adherence to authority (chap. 7),
   1. Bad authorities who have directly promoted error (chap. 8),
   2. Bad authorities who have indirectly promoted error (chap. 9).
Summary: How these three causes of error are "promoted" by Satan (chaps. 10–11). (Some critics have accused Browne of making Satan a "cause of error, but like the devil in all of us, he is only a "promoter" of error.)

The most apparent principle in the ordering of these three causes is chronological: from the initial fall of man to our credulous resort to the latest source of misdirection. In time this goes from natural to artificial: from the "rude heads" to those "improved by wisdom." Browne blames wiser heads more than he blames simple country folk as he blames Adam more than he does Eve: "Strange effects are naturally taken for miracles by weaker heads, and artificially improved to that [false] apprehension by wiser" (2. 6).[2] Ironically error is thus compounded by history.

More ironic is the principle that arranges these causes of error obversely in relation to the determinators of truth (which we shall soon examine): authority, reason, and experiment. By our initial disobedience we surrender the only real authority, God, and cling to a host of human "authorities" instead of diligently applying reason and ocular proof to God's other manuscript, Nature. As reason is the central of the three criteria for truth, so its opposite, verbal and logical fallacy, is the central of the three causes of error.

Under this lies an order of increasing heinousness and consequently increasing responsibility. Browne begins with the cause we are least responsible for, being children of Adam. More blameworthy is our susceptibility for delusion. But "the mortallest enemy unto knowledge" is the obstinate clinging to authority and to antiquity. This implies an increasing area of choice, for our responsibility increases as we pass from that cause which comes from outside ourselves, through the causes within ourselves, to the causes among ourselves. Or, to paraphrase Browne's central metaphor, the disease of error is partially *congenital,* very *self-infectious,* and dangerously *contagious.*

The deepest irony, however, comes as the final principle of arrangement of these three causes of error in the most subtly reasoned segment of book 1, the chapters on Satan. It were "too bold an arithmetic" to count all his wiles; therefore Browne contents himself with "what most considerably concerneth his popular and practised ways of delusion": deceiving mankind in five main points concerning himself and God, the force for truth which Satan rebels against. These five points are summarized in a single paragraph (1.10) like this:

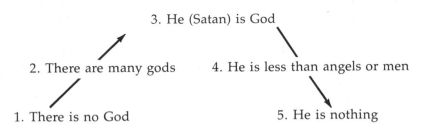

3. He (Satan) is God

2. There are many gods   4. He is less than angels or men

1. There is no God   5. He is nothing

Satan's five glozing propositions are arranged with the arch-sin of pride at the top. On either side are two pairs of minor propositions, a negative and positive leading up to it; and on the other side a positive and negative leading away from it.

Satin "promotes" error by attacking the "cure" of the epidemic, which we shall have to take up now. It has often been noticed how many chapters treat a subject first by the *authority* for or against a popular opinion; then by the application of *reason;* and finally, wherever feasible, by *experimentation* or ocular proof. Thus the most notorious chapter of all, the one on the badger, solemnly declares: "Upon enquiry I find . . . [the notion that its legs are longer on one side than on the other] repugnant unto the three Determinators of Truth, Authority, Sense, and Reason" (3.5). Similarly, the assertion that chameleons feed on air is "mainly controvertible, and . . . fails[s] in the three inducements of belief" (3.21). By his five propositions the devil overthrows in us the three determinators of truth. At both ends he denies the *authority* of God and of himself; in the middle he denies *reason* by denying the hierarchy of values; and in the very center, by setting himself above God, he denies *authority* and *reason* and his own *experiment.*

But far more often the three "cures for error" or "determinators of truth" are reduced to two. "Authority" tends to disappear, not because Browne is forgetful but because in science "reason" and "ocular proof" *are* the authority. There is only one final authority: "In brief, there is nothing infallible but GOD, who cannot possibly Erre" (1. 1). The first cause (original sin) and the first cure (God's authority) are put on one side, and the other two causes (fallacious reasoning and supinity) with their two cures (reason and experiment) are put on the other. There was precedent for this in Galen's *De sanitate tuenda* and many medical treatises: causes and cures of diseases are *either* outside *or* within man's power to control. Were Browne not to divide his causes and cures like this, the disease of error in his title would have had to be *endemic* rather than *epidemic,* and his treatment more religious than philosophical. Thus the first citation of the double rather than the triple criteria for truth comes as early as the very first paragraph of his preface: "proposing not only a large and copious List, but from *experience* and *reason* attempting their decisions." Hence Browne can take "the new and noble doctrine of the circulation of the blood" (4. 4) as well as "that excellent discourse *of Generation*" as authority because Harvey's validity in these two works is "So strongly erected upon the two great pillars of truth, experience and solid reason" (3.28). The determinators of truth are throughout the work applied to the causes of error.

On this epistemological foundation rest the following six books of error in (1) geology and botany, (2) zoology, (3) human anatomy and physiology, (4) customs of mankind, some depicted in art, (5) cosmology and history, and finally (6) interpretation of Scripture. The books follow the chronological order of the creation, from the earth of minerals and vegetables, through animals, to man; followed by man's works. Thus they go from natural to artificial, from God's clear design to the complex muddles of human history. This is an order from the apparently simple but actually complex to the apparently complex but actually simple. The books pass from that which can be seen and yet misunderstood by the common people to that which has been thought but grossly confounded by the wiser. Real authority, founded in reason and experiment, is most easily established in the areas of the first three books and becomes more difficult to attain as we proceed.

It is time now to take a few typical cases of error and see how Browne applies to them the determinators of truth—authority, reason, and experiment. Most human authority is dubious: "An argument from Authority," Browne declares, " . . . is but a topical probation . . . depending upon a naked asseveration: wherein neither declaring the causes, affections or adjuncts of what we believe, it carrieth not with it the reasonable inducements of knowledge" (1. 7). Such authority cannot be used at all in mathematics, only a little in natural philosophy, but "in Morality, Rhetorick, Law and History, there is I confess a frequent and allowable use of testimony." (1. 7). The worst authorities are those who write of events without eyewitnessing them, who confuse fact with myth, and in the whole process become magisterial (6. 6).

Browne would have us examine the grounds of all the "authorities" he cites for or against various propositions. For him, naturally, doctors have the best grounds. A Spanish physician, Franciscus Bustamentinus, won his credence about the animals in Scripture (3.16). And a group of doctors, like Sextius, Dioscorides, Galen, Matthiolus, spoke authoritatively sbout the salamander (3.14). But some doctors are guilty of deliberately gulling their patients (1.3). Other doctors make false deductions arising from ignorance of etymology (2.7); Cardan is caught red-handed (3.17), as well as many others. Yet every "authority" (in the sense of Aristotle the biologist, Pliny, or Galen) whose "authority" (in the sense of validity) shifts with the advance of science is measured by Browne in the same way as our "authorities" (Newton, Darwin, Einstein) are measured by us. Hence, as we have already discovered, authority tends to give way as a criterion of truth to the two major criteria: reason and observation.

Reason as a determinator of truth is applied to popular errors arising from the second cause of error, false inference. A good example is "deuteroscopy" or "the second intention of words" (1.3). A right rule for distinguishing between literal and poetic statements, for example in the macrocosm-microcosm conceit, "is beyond the subtlety of sense, and requires the artifice of reason," which puts it in a different class from the speed of light. In areas of knowledge where experiment cannot determine, Browne insists upon two kinds of truth, literal and emblematic. As a lack of anatomical knowledge through observation gave birth to many an emblem, so the failure to read the emblem aright has compounded the failures of observation into failures of understanding: for example, a pigeon has no gall, and therefore it is the symbol of peace; since it is the symbol of peace, it has no gall (3.3).

They lack reason who "apprehend a veritable history in an Emblem or piece of Christian poesy" and at the same time fail to perceive its poetic truth (5.17). A griffin, "countenanced by the Name sometimes found in Scripture and . . . and Hieroglyphick of the Egyptians," had "allowable morality" though no existence in zoology (3.11). The pelican's slashing her breast to feed her young with blood was "asserted by many holy Writers and was an Hieroglyphick of piety and pitty among the Ægytians" (5.1); its emblematic meaning is "safe," but taken literally of course, it is a vulgar error. A literal interpretation of Nicander's myth of vipers at birth tearing through their mother's bowels is an error, though the hieroglyphic meaning based on it of Christ's "generation of vipers" is true (3.16). A metaphor is a metaphor and a fact is a fact, and those who fail in the second determinator of truth, reason, wallow in that second cause of error, false inference, by mythologizing fact and factualizing myth, as for example in the story of Friar Bacon and Brasenose College, Oxford (7.17).

As poetic license may serve truth, *licentia pictoria* (5.11) often misleads; and Browne's devoting half of book 5 to mistakes in pictures, many of which he must have seen during vacations from medical study at Padua, arises from their two kinds of truth. Art which presumes to imitate nature must represent it "true"; otherwise, artists "may delineate old Nestor like Adonis, Hecuba with Helen's face, and Time with Absolon's head" (5.11). Browne would rather have Adam and Eve painted without navels. Pictorial emblems can mislead people; for example, "Poppy hath obtained the Epithite of fruitful, and . . . fertility was Hieroglyphically described by Venus with an head of Poppy in her hand; the reason hereof was the multitude of seed within itself, and no such multiplying in humane generation" (7.7). Poppy is a symbol, not an aphrodisiac. A devout reader of the Bible, Browne will not take its face value for history and natural science. To most of its passages he applies the same kind of reasoning that he applies to emblems, poetry, and myth: "And if we shall take it literally what Moses described popularly" (6.2), we fall victims to the epidemic. As for such accounts in secular history as Hannibal's eating his way through the Alps with strong vinegar, "yet may all be salved, if we take it hyperbolically," as wise men interpret certain passages in the Book of Job (7.18). He knew by deuteroscopy the two kinds of language and brought both to bear upon his religion: to describe nature exactly, "it may be literally said of the wisdom of God, what men will have but figuratively spoken of the works of Christ; that if the wonders thereof were duly described, the whole world, that is, all within the last circumference, would not contain them. for as his Wisdom is infinite, so cannot the due expressions thereof be finite." (6.5). Thus reason, the central determinator of truth, is shared by being applicable on the one hand to emblem, poetry, and religion, and, on the other, to things of sense.

But the third and last determinator of truth (ocular proof and demonstration through actual trial) is as limited in its way to things as the first, absolute authority, is limited in its way to God. Laughingly, Browne will admit that one advantage of vulgar errors is that they stir men like himself to experiment (7.18). Dogs of various shapes, breeds, and sizes apparently had the run of the house. He fed them finely pulverized glass with no ill effects (2.5), and even small doses of poisons (2.7). That puppies are blind nine days he finds "not answerable unto experience," for "upon strict observation of many" he discovered that Aristotle was right in seeking here a relationship with the period of gestation (3.27). On his laboratory scales registering one-tenth of a grain (4.7) he weighed the brains of a snipe to determine the relationship between the size of the brain and the body (4.2); and he strangled a chicken on the scales to discover whether it weighed more dead than alive (4.7). He counted over seven hundred stones in the gizzard of a turkey (3.22). He drowned cats, mice, and other animals to discover that their bodies floated to the surface at different times. He loved to float woods, metals, gems, and needles in various receptacles of water, quicksilver, aqua fortis, or brine. He dissected every kind of animal, from an earthworm (3.27) to a horse (3.2). He placed spiders and a toad in a jar together and found no "natural antipathy"; the toad placidly let the spiders crawl all over its head (3.27). One time a bee settled on the desk and he placed his finger on its diaphragm to feel it hum (3.17). Collecting deathwatch beetles from the wainscoting of his house, he counted and described their ticking sounds made with a proboscis like a tiny woodpecker's—no one in his family died as a result (2.7). His experiments with electricity and magnetic bodies were ceaseless, even to discrediting (with needless work, it seems) a fancy method of sending written messages by magnetical sympathy (2.3).

Browne was a practicing physician and (primarily) a biologist. Hence he applies most carefully his ocular proof to vulgar error in those areas closest to his profession—generation, metabolism, and death; or sex, growth, and decay. In these matters, at once the least and the greatest experiences of our human lot, there is no hint of the virtuoso. In his embryological experiments with chicken eggs his instinct for Aristotle and for Christian teleology led him to epigenesis rather than the more modish theory of preformation, and he was scientifically right.[3]

As a biologist Browne was fascinated by sex as he was aware of the multiplicity of its vulgar errors. Country contraceptives abounded, like the left testicle of a weasel wrapped in a piece of she-mule hide (1.7). It was believed that to bring on menstruation a woman could urinate on earth newly cast up by a mole (5.23). Almost every plant in the pharmacopoeia of the day was held by someone to be either a promoter of venery or its opposite. There was the sexual nonsense of the mandrake root (2.6), and people said that the lodestone was an aphrodisiac (2.3). As for opium, Browne is inclined to believe those who say its effect "is not so much to invigorate themselves in coition, as to . . . spin out the motions of carnality" (7.7).

Living just before the determination of sex in plants, Browne noted that though sex is single in trees, animal generation requires two sexes. He concedes double sex in some creatures, and transference from one sex to the other in hares and even in humans (3.17). But since God created most living creatures male and female, patiently the doctor watches cocks treading hens (2.7). From an examination of the genitals he deduced that elephants copulate not like camels (as Pliny said they did) but by supersaliency, like horses (3.1). He lists the size, shape, and position of a variety of pizzles, including one of a deer distended and covered with flies, but not rotting as the natives believed (3.9). Ignorance of the anatomy of genitalia accounted for the many mistakings of the anal glands for the testicles in beavers, badgers, and hares, giving rise to home-spun theories of generation contrary to the laws of nature, reason, and God (3.4). As part of these laws he lists every physiologically possible position in coitus (3.17).

From the mystery of generation and growth, Browne turned his observation to the facts of decay. Throughout *Vulgar Errors* ring solemn words on death, like these on the conceit of man's immortality on earth, which anticipate *Urn Burial*: "Some indeed have been so affectedly vain, as to counterfeit Immortality, and have stoln their death, in a hope to be esteemed immortal; and others have conceived themselves dead; but surely few or none have fallen upon so bold an errour, as not to think that they could die at all. Surely although delusion may run high, and possible it is that for a while a man may forget his nature, yet cannot this be durable. For the unconcealable imperfections of ourselves, or their daily examples in others, will hourly prompt us our corruption, and loudly tell us we are the sons of earth" (7.10). Thus the application of the last determinator of truth, observation and experiment, is brought full circle to the first great cause of error, our inherited and common infirmity.

There emerges from Browne's *Vulgar Errors* the portrait of a man who is charitable in his opinions because he is wise in anthropology, humorous in his intellectual detachment, and devout in his religion. The instinct that led him at the age of thirty to begin the second part of *Religio* with "Now for that other virtue of charity" had been proved from 1635 to 1645 by his sensible and rational experience; intellectually he had to assent to Christ's authoritative second commandment to love thy neighbor as thyself. Browne is charitable toward Jews and Negroes not out of sentiment but out of science. That the shape of a nose or the color of a skin is a deformity is a terrifyingly unfounded opinion (cf. 6. 11. 247); and Jews do not stink because they crucified Christ, nor are Negroes black because of the sun or because of a curse on one of the tribes of Israel. Browne's quiet skepticism is equally applied to two-headed snakes and the "repugnancy" of rejected nations.

Therefore the humor running throughout *Vulgar Errors* is, like all real humor, a rational detachment from self which can criticise with love. His humor ranges from puns to sarcasm. To be governed by the canicular days is "to suffer from the mouth of the Dog above, what others do from the teeth of the Dogs below" (4.13). "Curiosity *fruitlessly* enquireth" about the apple Eve is supposed to have plucked (7.1). Into a serious description of asbestos he introduces two popular incombustibles, Germanicus's heart and Pyrrhus's big toe (3.14). To admit that elephants can walk and yet deny them joints in their legs "were to expect a Race from Hercules his pillars; or hope to behold the effects of Orpheus his Harp, when trees found joints, and danced after his Musick" (3.1). And the story of a woman who got pregnant from taking a bath he calls "a new and unseconded way in History to fornicate at a distance" (7.16). Browne loves to reduce proverbs to their essential absurdity, especially those which, if taken seriously, violate everyday experience. If Rome were built in a day, this is "an Art quite lost with our Mechanicks" (7.17). Imputing to a plant like Ethiopian mullein the virtue of opening any lock would "condemn the judgment of Scipio, who having such a picklock, would spend so many years in battering the Gates of Carthage" (2.6).

Lightened as it is by humor, *Vulgar Errors* is also the work of a devoutly humble inquirer after truth. English prose like this (rare in most works of popular science) must be read aloud:

> For unto God a thousand years are no more than one moment, and in his sight Methuselah lived no nearer one day than Abel, for all parts of time are alike unto him, unto whom none are referrible; and all things present, unto whom nothing is past or to come. And therefore, although we be measured by the Zone of time, and the flowing and

continued instants thereof, do weave at last a line and
circle about the eldest: yet can we not thus commensurate
the sphere of Trismegistus; or sum up the unsuccessive
and stable duration of God. [7.3]

No longer are we inclined to believed that Satan, having been
silenced in the oracles, still speaks in witches and poltergeists, yet
if we have substituted new errors for old, it may be as true now as
it was in 1645 to say with Browne: "In vain we cry that Oracles are
down; Apollo's Altar still doth smoak; nor is the fire of Delphos
out unto this day" (7.12). Nor will it be perhaps until the day of
judgment when "men shall rise out of the earth: the graves shall
shoot up their concealed seeds, and in that great Autumn, men
shall spring up, and awake from their Chaos again" (6.1).

Meanwhile, Browne's book on the human disease of error and
how to inoculate ourselves against it may help us reduce the
mental and moral chaos of our own lives.

10 Why Listen to a Seventeenth-Century Funeral Sermon?

Among the thousands of sermons printed in England during the seventeenth century, the funeral sermon ranks high both in number and in homiletic excellence. Its elements differ more by degree than by kind from those of its every-Sunday cousin or the Gunpowder special occasion. It deserves separate treatment because of its history, its contribution to the period's preoccupation with death, its highly developed structure and style, and its relationship to the art of biography.

One should not compare English funeral sermons with the great funeral orations of Bossuet, as Matthew Arnold, for one, does (see below, p. 127). In France, the *oraison funèbre* is a separate genre and has its numerous definers, like Villeman, Thomas, la Harpe, Maury, and Dessault; few have written on the English funeral sermon. Moreover, in Bossuet the dead are kings, queens, and *maréchaux;* in England, they are parishioners and most often brothers of the cloth, whether vicar or bishop. Villeman's two kinds of French sermons are (1) "le sermon qui s'occupe des mystères de la foi, et des règles de la moral evangelique"; (2) l'oraison funèbre qui celèbre et consacre les grandes virtues humaines."[1] The *oraison funèbre* is extravagant in eulogy; it emphasizes loss, often with tears. The English sermon subordinates eulogy and rejoices in heavenly gain. In England, the funeral sermon has

This essay appeared embryologically in the *Anglican Theological Review* (Evanston, Ill.) 38 (1956): 226–34. A redaction was read as a paper at the Conference of Christianity and Literature at Normal, Illinois, April 1980.

always been a sermon whose special theme is immortality, as in
the Prayer Book service for the burial of the dead. The *oraison
funèbre*, on the other hand, is classical; its models are Thucydides'
speech put into the mouth of Pericles, the orations of De-
mosthenes, and the panegyrics of Cicero. The English funeral
sermon finds it origin in the church fathers, particularly Gregory
Nazianzus and Basil; it is not panegyric but homily. The life and
character of the deceased become not the backbone of the speech
but merely a final exemplum of well-earned eternal life through
bodily death. A seventeenth-century witness to the distinction is
the Reverend Richard Harris in his 1618 funeral sermon for Sir
Anthony Cope; avoiding excessive praise of the deceased, he says
in his "Epistle to the Reader": "I could wish, that our age would
distinguish betwixt funerall Orations, and funerall Sermons, as
former ages have done, and not confound so different things."[2]

There are funeral *sermons* in French and funeral *orations* in English, and yet the distinction is clear. The funeral book published
in Aberdeen in 1635 on the death of Bishop Patrick Forbes[3] contains a Latin *oratio funebris,* an English funeral oration, and several
funeral sermons side by side. The orations have no biblical text
and are practically all eulogy. But the Reverend Robert Baron's
sermon, based on Revelation 14:13 for fifty-one pages, introduces
the last seven pages with: "Having gone through my Text, I now
apply myselfe, and my Text both, to this present Text, which lyeth
before us: I mean, the dead halfe of our late most worthie, and
Reverend, and now most blessed Prelate." In the same volume Dr.
William Guild's sermon expands the theme from Luke 2:29 for
twenty-one pages, and in the last two pages compares the dead
bishop to Simeon uttering the *Nunc dimittis.*

The funeral sermon had a rhetorical advantage in its occasion.
For the living it held some of the macabre appeal of the last words
of a dying man. Donne's own funeral sermon became his best
known. Archbishop Laud's sermon on the block was hawked about
before the ink and blood were dry.[4] Taylor's swan song was his
funeral sermon for Archbishop Bramhall, lord primate of Ireland.
The only sermon of Bunyan we possess is his "last sermon," delivered in a fever on 19 August 1688. Gilbert Burnett, whose fine
funeral sermons and skill in biography may be related (he detested
funeral orations), tells us in his *Life and Death of Sir Matthew Hale*

that the famous judge's speeches to condemned prisoners "directing them to prepare for death were so Weighty, so free from all Affectation, and so Serious and Devout, that many loved to go to the Tryals when he sate Judg, to be edified by his Speeches, and behaviour in them, and used to say *they heard very few such Sermons.*"[5] Witness the Reverend William Lloyd's opening at the funeral of Bishop John Wilkins:

> In handling the text of holy Scriptures [Heb. 13:7], that we mingle nothing of Human Affections, that our Passions may give no Interruption to you in hearing, or to me in speaking; I should desire to suppress them quite, if it were possible. And possible it is, where they are slightly raised, as upon common and ordinary Occasions: But where they are grounded and strong, where they dare argue, and seem to have reason on their side, as there is too much in sight for ours; there I think it is vain to endeavour it. The only way in this Case, is to give them some kind of Vent, to discharge them in part, and to govern what remains of the Affections.[6]

A controlled piece of prose on the occasion of a funeral adds to the edification of a sermon the catharsis of high tragedy.

Even the drama of death could not excuse a preacher's failure to satisfy in his structure and style the strict demands of a sermon. As Bishop Wilkins wrote in his *Ars predicandi* (1646): "There are two abilities requisite in every one that will teach and instruct another: . . . A right understanding of sound doctrine, and to affirm, and apply it unto edification of others."[7] This double purpose of exposition and application has accounted through the centuries for the shape that most sermons take—from the announcing of the text, through the explanation of the text, to the application of the new-found meaning to men's lives. The funeral sermon had two additional minor ends: the appropriate justification of the deceased's life and the consolation of the bereaved.[8]

If the main purpose is to edify, then the best sermons are those which declare the essential teachings of Christianity, and there is no more essential doctrine than the paradox of Easter, the ultimate assertion of victory over death. Such a theme for a funeral sermon has not changed since the medieval *Craft of Dying*, whose purpose was to teach all men of Christian faith that by dying in certain hope of a resurrection they most imitate Christ.[9] By virtue of this central theme, funeral sermons in the seventeenth century achieved a logical control over their structure and style that later in the century became ideal—quite different from the verbal dissections of some of Launcelot Andrewes's sermons or the medieval chop-logic of some of Donne's.

A Restoration example is the sermon (no. 24) by Archbishop Tillotson, preached at the funeral of Benjamin Whichcote on 24 May 1683.[10] The thesis of life through death, appropriate at the funeral of a Christian Neo-platonist, is served by Corinthians 5:6—"Wherefore we are always confident, knowing that whilst we are at home in the body we are absent from the Lord." These words," continues Tillotson, "contain one of the chief grounds of encouragement which the Christian Religion gives us against the Fear of Death."[11] In the next three pages he puts this text in its context, and ends with five "useful corollaries." His explication finished, he turns to the application in the life of the deceased. After giving the biographical facts and drawing a "character" of Whichcote which fits the theme, the text, and the explication, he comes to the exordium: "And now methinks the Consideration of the Argument I have been upon and of that great Example that is before us, should raise our Minds above this World, and fix them upon the Glory and Happiness of the other."

A biography of Whichcote in a rhetorically effective religious argument raises another question besides that of cogency, the question of truth. How trustworthy is it as biography? About 1642 the learned John Selden gave his opinion: "For a man to say all the excellent things that can be said upon one, and call that his epitaph, 'tis as if a painter should make the handsomest piece that he can possibly make, and say 'twas my picture. It holds in a funeral sermon."[12] Dr. Johnson was aware of the problem. He begins his "Life of Cowley" by saying that the "zeal of friendship, or ambition of eloquence" of Dr. Sprat, the preceding biographer of Cowley, "has produced a funeral oration [not funeral sermon] rather than a history: ... for he writes with so little detail that ... all is shown confused and enlarged through the mist of panegyrick." Both preachers and congregations were aware of the danger of hyperbole, despite the fact that the reputation of the preacher, a knowledgeable audience, and the very structure of an

English funeral sermon all limited the too-free imagination and the too-passionate bias. Richard Baxter on John Corbet said at the end of his exemplum:

> Some will think that in partiality I over-magnifie men, because they are of my own mind and party: I have (besides some pious Women) written the Characters, and published the praises of divers men . . . [he lists them]: and he that hath now received them, whom such as you cast out or Villified, knoweth that I have in knowledge of them, and love to Christ, whose grace shined in them, spoken simply the truth from my heart; and it is in a time and place where it is fully known, and feareth no confutation. [13]

Again, the Rev. Robert Baron in his 1635 funeral sermon on Bishop Forbes of Aberdeen comes to the end of his "character" with a conscious check: "Lest my speaches seeme to those who knew him not, and so loved him not, to proceede from a flattering humour, I will not say of him as Velleius Paterculus sayde of Scipio Æmilianus [*Hist. Rom.* 1.1] that in all his lyfe he neyther did, nor spake, nor thought anie thing, but that which was prayse worthie (a speech not hyperbolicke onlie but impious)." [14] The classical comparison reminds us again that a Christian funeral sermon is distinct from an *oratio funebris;* it assumes all men to be sinners open to grace.

   If the preacher is not bound by his religion or by the solemnity of the occasion to speak the truth in his "character" of the deceased, the audience are natural checks, though they may wish to hear only the good. Again, Burnett wrote of Sir Matthew Hale: "But there is great encouragement in this, that I write concerning a Man so fresh in all Peoples Remembrance, that is so lately Dead, and was so much and so well known, that I shall have many Vouchers, who will be ready to justifie me in all that I am to relate, and to add a great deal to what I can say." [15] The validity of "characters" in funeral sermons was sometimes attacked by members of the opposing ecclesiastical party. An example is *Some Discourses upon Dr. Burnett and Dr. Tillotson, Ocassioned by the Late Funeral Sermon of the Latter* (London, 1695), attributed to Dr. George Hickes. After destroying the character that Burnett, the "Encomiast," gives of Tillotson, Hickes concludes that clergymen (he probably means

Anglican clergymen) ought to avoid in funeral sermons the appearance of biographical prevarication: "We have had of late so many fulsome and despicable Sermons of Flattery as no Age ever saw, or will I hope see again."

It is equally possible for an Anglican to accuse a Presbyterian of grossly flattering his subject. But remembering that we are reading funeral sermons and not *oraisons funèbres*, and that the preacher and the deceased are well known to the congregation, there seems to be little reason for doubting the biographical facts contained in the exempla of seventeenth-century funeral sermons. A complete index of seventeenth-century printed and manuscript funeral sermons, by the names of the deceased, the names of the preachers, and the geographical location by counties would be useful for the historian and literary biographer. Note how often a funeral sermon is listed among the sources in the DNB. With a computer, the project now seems more nearly within some one's reach. Although Mrs. Lewalski is quite right in pointing out that many of the personal exempla at the ends of funeral sermons are practically the same, inasmuch as they are symbols of the life of a true Christian who believed himself to be made in the image of God, nevertheless an exemplum may contain such valuable biographical information as the name of the college and tutors, the friends, the travels, and the recreations of the deceased.

The seventeenth-century funeral sermon often marked the highest achievement of its preachers, particularly in the Anglican church. Its history as homily rather than encomium, the drama of its occasion, the cogency of its structure, and the validity of its exempla—all to assert the Christian theme of life in the challenging presence of death—make for pulpit eloquence. The best sermon of Taylor is the sermon on the countess of Carberry; of Bishop Rust, his sermon on Taylor; of Tillotson, the sermon on Whichcote; and of Burnett, the sermon on Tillotson.[16]

11   Jeremy Taylor versus "Total Depravity"

Repentance is the most pervasisve doctrine in the whole of Jeremy Taylor's writings—polemical, devotional, homiletic, and casuistical. One reason for this is that he shared with many in the seventeenth century, which opened with Hamlet's "The time is out of joint," an eschatological feeling that the world is drawing toward its end. "'Tis too late to be ambitious," sighed Dr. Thomas Browne. Upon the defeat of the Loyalist and the Anglican cause, Taylor sought to get back to first things, which is man's sin and the hope of redemption—like Isaiah and John the Baptist and Savonarola in similar periods of decay. To Taylor this was eminently practical. Even at so divisive a time as that of civil war, repentance is something we can do immediately; it is the practice of faith. At the crisis of his life and of his country, he wrote *Unum Necessarium; or, The Doctrine and Practice of Repentance, Describing the Necessities and Measures of a Strict, a Holy, and a Christian Life, and Rescued from Popular Errors* (1655). Central to its doctrine is the controversy in which he hazarded his career, his personal liberty, and even his life, the controversy on original sin. There had been books in his time on "popular errors" in medicine, history,

---

This essay is distilled from my fifty-two page chapter 4 of *Jeremy Taylor and the Great Rebellion: A Study of His Mind and Temper in Controversy* (Ann Arbor: University of Michigan Press, 1970). Most of the citations of Taylor are made to *The Whole Works of the Right Reverend Jeremy Taylor ... by the Right Reverend Reginald Heber ... Revised and Corrected by the Rev. Charles Page Eden*, 10 vols. (London, 1852–61).

botany, and zoology; the unifying "popular error" of the title of this religious book by Taylor is the doctrine of total depravity.

The argument is heralded by a simple story from the Gospel of Luke (10:38 ff.) that has a domestic setting and rings with essential truth, a story he had already used effectively in *The Liberty of Prophesying*. It is the story of how Mary had chosen "the one thing needful" while her sister Martha did the kitchen chores. What is that one thing needful, *unum necessarium*, except to listen to the words of the Master? And if we listen, what is the word we hear? In 1655 Taylor wagered his life on this answer: What Jesus says to all who listen is that he came into this world to save us from our sins; and in return he requires of us repentance. The Presbyterian party in power emphasized original sin, reprobation, and limited atonement. Taylor's succinct reaction is: you cannot repent of a sin you have not committed; repent of your own, not Adam's. If Calvinistic "original sin" stands in the way of true repentance, as Taylor was convinced it does, he must set out boldly to destroy the doctrine so that we can help God go about his real business here on earth.

The doctrine of original sin must begin with man's first consciousness of evil in the world.[1] Why is it that most men know that love and wisdom and justice are palpable goods experientially arrived at, and yet rule their lives and the lives of others by hate, stupidity, and extortion? Greek tragedy, especially that of Aeschylus, broods on this dark theme.

For the Hebraic-Christian view of life, the existential fact of sin is given mythically in the story of Adam and Eve and the murder of their son Abel by his own brother Cain. Christian theologians early found here hints of either a total depravity or else an imputation of guilt. As the concept developed in Jewish thought, however, the individual alone is responsible for giving in to his own evil imagination: for example, Ezekiel 18:4—"Behold, all souls are mine:as the soul of the father, so also the soul of the son is mine; the soul that sinneth, it shall die." In the New Testament Saint Paul first gives it extended treatment, but Saint Paul's ideas in Romans, the *locus classicus* for Christians, have accommodated innumerable and conflicting interpretations. What is the mediating link between Adam's sin and death in us? Seminal existence as hinted at in Hebrews 7:9ff.? In Romans, does Paul refer our sin to Adam's in the sense that Christians "die to sin," that is, merely in a metaphorical or typological sense? One thing that emerges from the commentaries on Romans throughout the history of Christian thinking is that many have taken literally such metaphors as that of the potter and the pots (Rom. 9:21).

Starting from the Jewish and Pauline doctrines, the early church fathers divided into what might be called the "soft" and the "hard" schools. Gentle Origen, for example, began by treating the biblical narrative as allegory of souls in a Phaedrus-like pre-existence, so that original sin is derived not from Adam but from each person's individual will. An even "softer" father was the second-century Tatian, in whose *Apology* first appears the concept of "original righteousness," later taken up by Duns Scotus. "Original sin" becomes, then, merely the deprivation of the supernatural gift of grace enjoyed by prelapsarian man, and not the cause, from Adam's disobedience, of an irrevocably dislocated human nature.

The necessity to confute the Pelagian heresy turned Saint Augustine into the "hardest" church father on the subject of original sin. Where orthodox Christianity depends on synergism, or the dualistic thrust of both God and man, Pelagius and his followers set man up so high as to make God almost unnecessary. To prove how incapable man is by himself, Augustine, particularly in *De peccato originali*, had to argue that man is born a sinner as he is born in Adam, a theory that adumbrates John Calvin.

At the Council of Dort (1617–18), the "soft" pleas of the Remonstrants for that kind of *recta ratio* which underlies Hooker's Anglicanism fell before the "hard" arguments used by the theologians from Geneva, sent to Dortrecht in Holland for the great debate. The English delegates represented rather King James than the English church, though as Anglicans they had all sworn to uphold the Thirty-nine Articles. James, as a Scottish theologian himself, sided with the Calvin-Knox thinking of Franz Gomarus (1563–1641), the Dutch "reformed" professor who opposed the liberal Remonstrants.[2] Led by Episcopius and Hugo Grotius, the anti-Calvin "Arminian" forces as Dort had prepared their arguments (in vain, it turned out) from such "soft" thinkers on original sin as Castellio and Arminius, forerunners of present-day liberal theology.[3]

That Taylor was steeped in Arminianism is shown by almost everything he wrote, and by his list of books for a theological library drawn up in 1660: in this list he singles out "Episcopius, whose whole works are excellent, and containe the whole body of orthodox religion" (*Works*, I: xxxix). But in England the fourth chapter of the *Directory for the Publique Worship of God*, entitled "Of the Fall of Man, and of Sin, and the Punishment Thereof," published in 1645 by the Westminister Assembly, is even "harder" than anything contained in Calvin's *Institutes*.

Taylor's argument against the concept of "total depravity" appears in a dozen documents, written between 1655 and 1658, some of them in his prison cell at Chepstow Castle. The grounds of his argument are the usual grounds of the Anglican apologist: Scripture, tradition, and reason, with reason applied to the interpretation of the the Bible and to the meaning of history. At the end of an extra chapter to *Unum Necessarium*, Taylor writes: "I hope I have done my duty, having produced scripture, and reasons, and the best authority" (7:340). As is usual in seventeenth-century Anglican argumentation, reason does not intend the close syllogistic brand of Aristotle and Saint Thomas, but a skepticism, a weighing of alternatives in the scale of common sense, a trust in the "more probable," and an appeal to most right-thinking men in a "Platonic" not-only-but-also dialectic. Right reason is intelligence augmented by ethics, religion, and good sense. Thus Taylor declares his grounds to be "Scripture and right reason, and the doctrine of the primitive church for the first three hundred years" (p. 19), that is, before Augustine. To Bishop Warner he asserts: "In this I have not only scripture and all the reason of the world on my side, but the complying sentences of the most eminent writers of the primitive church" (p. 565). Reexamining Saint Paul's theories of original sin, he proposes to "separate the certain from the uncertain, that which is revealed from that which is presumed, that which is reasonable from that which makes too bold reflections upon God's honour, and the reputation of His justice and His goodness" (p. 244). Taylor wonders why Calvinists insist on "difficult" and "obscure" passages in Saint Paul to "prove" determinism and overlook so clear a statement on freedom as 1 Corinthians 7:37: "He that standeth steadfast in his heart, having no necessity, but hath power over his own will, and hath so decreed in his heart . . . [he] doeth well." Thus the three grounds of right reason, the Bible, and the authority of history overlap and intertwine, sometimes one emerging as more important, sometimes another, but still standing firm in the court of every appeal.

On these grounds Taylor raised three main arguments: the argument of truth, the argument of ethics, and the argument of religion. In the first, being a learned man, he is not interested in mere custom but in actual truth (if he can find it) of biblical interpretation, history, and human psychology. In the second, being a practical man, he fights for those views on the problem of original sin which make individual men better and societies peaceful. In the third, being a pious and devoted Christian, he speaks for those views which add to the greater glory of God. The usual doctrines of original sin, he asserts, are false, inimical to good behavior, and dishonorable to God's goodness and justice. Taylor's views, on the contrary, would have to be true, workable, and holy. These are close to the three criteria for knowledge which Milton's Raphael sets for his inquisitive student Adam in the Garden of Eden. Adam can know those things which (1) are within his capacity to know—"what thou canst attain"; (2) which "infer thee also happier"; and (3) which "best may serve to glorify the Maker" (*P.L.*, 7. 115–20).

Certainly the first problem must be the "truth" in Adam's fall. Is it true that we inherit that "original" sin and thus are guilty of it? Adam in the great Hebrew myth was punished for the first disobedience. Punishment is usually thought of as a deprivation of something which the sinning person once possessed. The truth of the story in Genesis, Taylor believes, is that Adam at creation had a natural grace, a *superadditum* which God justly took away from him as punishment. As a result natural man (and we inherit Adam's nature) cannot by his own strength arrive at a supernatural end; so that grace, after the fall, became a conditioned gift. All that the Bible tells us clearly is that we have received more by the "second Adam," Christ, than we lost by the first. In view of the charges hurled at Taylor of Pelagianism, it must be clear that where the Pelagians asserted that Adam's fall does not involve mankind, Taylor insists that it does. Among his many statements to this effect, we need quote only one now, at the beginning of *Deus Justificatus:* "But first, . . . be pleased to remember that the question is not whether there be any such thing as original sin; for it is certain and confessed on all hands almost. For my part, I cannot but confess that to be which I feel, and groan under, and by which all the world is miserable" (7:497). And where the Pelagians were "heretical" in arguing that man is capable of perfection without divine grace, Taylor consistently argues that in God's economy our necessary dependence upon grace was purchased for us by Adam's obedience. Adam was created immortal. Forfeiting that gift, he was left in what Taylor calls his natural mortal state. His sin infected us with death, which we derive from our birth; that is, we too are born mortal and have to die. Even an infant, Saint Cyprian says, who has had no chance to sin, is mortal; and infant mortality cannot possibly be punishment for Adam's sin. Mortality is a condition of being born, but God through Christ has given us an opportunity to escape even this "law." Adam's sin then, hurts us, but it cannot damn us.

Let us invent a parable to illustrate Taylor's reasoning at this point. Suppose an American businessman, of good reputation in his community, is convicted of embezzlement, fined ten thousand dollars, and put into prison for ten years. As a result, his son, aged thirteen at the time, becomes emotionally disturbed and drops out of school. He is not being punished for his father's crime, nor has he committed a crime of his own. The condition of his life has been made a lot harder for him because of what his father did. But by dint of that handicap he may succeed even more than his father, especially if a benefactor, perceiving the boy's misfortune and promise, volunteers to "adopt" him. In this way, Taylor would argue, we are all the "sons" of Adam and of Christ. So much for the argument of truth, truth secured to Taylor mainly by the principles enunciated in *The Liberty of Prophesying* to bring right reason to bear upon the interpretation of the Bible.

His next argument is an ethical one: those views of original sin are best which allow us to live better lives. "Sin" in its theological context causes us to do "evil" in a social context. Like Milton, Taylor clings to free will and the consequent centrality of choice in the ethical life. Adam's sin does not bind us to continual evil; to think thus is self-deception and worse, self-excuse. Eve blamed the serpent, Adam blamed Eve, we blame Adam, but each consciously chose evil rather than good, and faced with the consequence sought self-exculpation. "Thou art deceived," Taylor quotes Seneca as saying (p. 263), "if thou thinkest that vices are born with us; no, they are superinduced and come in upon us afterwards."

Yet many attempt to prove that we are congentially evil by

quoting Psalm 51:5—"Behold, I was shapen in iniquity; and in sin did my mother conceive me." Taylor deplores the antisexuality in the many interpretations of this verse from the time of Saint Augustine to his own. To him sex is not sin and it is not evil: it may be part of the animality of man, but it is saved from carnality by love and marriage. David at that verse, Taylor believes, is being penitential, not self-exculpatory. "No man," he continues, "can perish for being an 'animal' man, that is for not having any supernatural revelations, but for not consenting to them when he hath, that is, for being 'carnal' as well as 'animal'; and that he is 'carnal' is wholly his own choice" (p. 269). Again, "A man is naturally inclined to desire the company of a woman whom he fancies," Taylor says. "This is naturally no sin: for the natural desire was put into us by God, and therefore could not be evil" (p. 277). Furthermore, inveterate Bible quoters take "shapen in iniquity" out of its Jewish context. It does not refer to original sin , for in the same psalm appear, before this verse, "Wash me thoroughly from mine iniquity, and cleanse me from my sin; for I acknowledge my transgressions, and my sin is ever before me" (verses 2–3), and, after the verse, one of Taylor's favorites, "The sacrifices of God are a broken spirit; a broken and contrite heart, O God, thou wilt not despise" (verse 17). Four times Taylor quotes this verse as the first step in individual repentance, since the ancient Jewish poem as a whole celebrates before God the individual's ethical responsibility for his own acts of mind and body.

If none of us is born evil, then this predilection we have for evil cannot be a consequence of Adam's sin. To be good all the time goes against our "nature": we are not built for perfect temperance, abstinence, patience, humility, self-denial, but have to strive for them—or else merely yield to our "condition."

Despite Adam, then, we can still choose to sin or not to sin, and among several goods or evils choose the greater or the less. The contrary would destroy all law, rewards and punishments. This is plainly biblical, too. After the fall, man "knew what nakedness was, and had experience of the difference of things; he perceived the evil and mischief of disobedience and the divine anger; he knew fear and flight, new apprehensions, and the trouble of a guilty conscience" (p. 279). Therefore, "to deny to the will of man powers of choice and election... destroys the [blissful] immortality of the soul" (p. 280).

Thus Taylor's ethical argument embraces a view of man's existentialist state. That we are born to suffer and to die is a condition of life, not a punishment for a sin we did not commit. He adds Pliny to Seneca as pagan witness to what we know from the Bible: "The creature . . . begins his life with punishments, for no fault, but that he was born" (p. 285). From an ethical point of view, lack of righteousness in ourselves is not a thing but a lack of a thing and hence is no sin. Concupiscence, similarly, is neither sin nor evil before we consent to it. Our spirit can do nothing without the miracle of grace, partly because of our natural impotency and partly because of our folly. For the first we have Jesus Christ, and of the second we cannot complain (p. 288).

The ethical argument is a strong one, since Taylor, reminded of "God's economy," is always practical. "That's a good repentance that bears fruit, and not that which produces leaves only," he wrote in another context:

> When the heathen gods were to choose what trees they
> would have sacred to them and used in their festivals,
> Jupiter chose the oak, Venus the myrtle, Apollo loved the
> laurel, but wise Minerva took the Olive . . . the Olive gives
> an excellent fruit, fit for food and physick, which when
> Jupiter observed, he kissed his daughter, and called her
> wise; for all pompousness is vain, and the solemn religion
> stands for nothing, unless that which we do, be profitable
> and good for material use. [9:20]

To believe that because of Adam we cannot help doing evil is to surrender ethical choice and with it the opportunity to repent of the sins which we, not Adam, commit, and thus to miss the opportunity to be forgiven for them.

This brings Taylor to his final and most important argument, not against original sin—he never denies the existence of original sin—but against the Calvinistic assumption of total depravity: it denigrates God's wisdom, justice, and love. A father himself and made even more sensitive to the ordinary human attachments within the family by successive deaths of his own children, Taylor is eloquent on the subject of the damnation of infants. "To condemn infants to hell for the fault of another," he cries, "is to deal worse with them than God did to the very devils, who did not perish but for an act of their own most perfect choice" (p. 255). And he caps his assertion that God does not damn anyone merely for the sin of our first father with a quotation from Saint Ambrose's commentary on Romans, chapter 5: *"Mors autem dissolutio corporis est . . . sed eius occasione propriis peccatis acquiretur*—death is the dividing soul and body; there is also another death which is in hell, and is called the second death, which we do not suffer for the sin of Adam, but by occasion of it we fall into it by our own sins" (p. 257).

Anticipating what in our time is called "guilt by association," Taylor argues for the honor of God in that he never imputes a sin to a whole race on account of the commission of sin by a single individual or group. God in the Old Testament may visit evil on a son as judge not of the son but of the father, but since Christ came, God surrended this right of dominion, for Christ came to plead for us; and here Taylor quotes the Latin of the Jewish Simeon Barsema which he found in Hugo Grotius's *De Jure Belli et Pacis* (p. 274).

Like Milton, then, Taylor must "justify the ways of God to man." Calvinistic doctrines of original sin, whether among most of the Presbyterians and Independents of his day or some of his fellow Anglicans, impute to God motives which it were a sin to impute to our fellow man. The worst doctrine is supralapsarianism, that God is pleased to damn persons even before they are born—like the Roman lictors who, not being allowed to execute virgins, ravished Sejanus's daughters so that they could legally murder them (p. 501). Supralapsarians make God out to be not good, not just, and not reasonable. The more wary and temperate Calvinists, such as the followers of Gomarus at the Council of Dort, assert that God reprobates most people but chooses a few others for salvation. Still other Calvinists, those at the Westminister Assembly, assert that corruption of nature remains even in the regenerate, and though it may be pardoned through Christ, still it is a sin which Adam's guilt has brought upon us all. The passion with which Taylor fought all these forms of Calvinism is shown in a sentence from *Deus Justificatus:* "I have, I confess, heartily opposed it, and shall, besides my arguments, *confute it with my blood, if God shall call me;* for it is so great a reproach to the Spirit and power of Christ, and to the effects of baptism, to scripture and to right reason, that all good people are bound in conscience to be zealous against it" (p. 508, my italics). Taylor must argue on religious grounds against those Anglicans who, though they agree with him that we inherit original righteousness, yet insist on Article 9 (in the Thirty-nine Articles of Religion) as part of the "Anglican creed." It is not. Article 9 was adopted in 1562 to make peace with the Calvinists against the Roman Catholics at a particular juncture in history; and the Thirty-nine Articles should be read and are read (since they form no part of worship) with the same spirit of latitude with which they were originally agreed upon. That Taylor dared to renounce Article 9, "of Original or Birth-Sin" seemed more heinous to Bishop Warner than anything else he said.

If it is intolerable to damn children for the sin of Adam (and Taylor's emphasis upon children throughout the controversy is not sentimental but theological—if God is in fact the Father), then it is intolerable that the sin itself be damnable, since sentence and execution are the same issue in God's justice. If by Adam we fall into a damnable condition, then when are we freed? At the time of our baptism? If so, anyone who dies before baptism must suffer eternal torment, and what kind of God visits this upon a child? Taylor believes that we are born free, so that we are never charged with that guilt: Christ came to save mankind, and Christ satisfies all sins, including Adam's. Only, and this is part of the essential synergistic principle, motivated by his grace we must of ourselves come to Christ even as Mary *chose* to sit at his feet to hear his word.

It is more probable (*probabilior*) that children should be born beloved and quitted of wrath than that they should be born hated and condemned in Adam. We would be foolish to honor a physician for curing us of a disease we never had, or praise the Father's mercy for wounding us in order that his Son may have the honor to bind up the wound. It is simply bad economy to make a necessity for the purpose of finding a remedy. It dishonors God to think he works this way. Taylor's Christian creed in all this is simple and would run like this: I believe that we are left natural by Adam, that Christ is revealed as having come to do for us what our nature cannot do by itself: give us a new birth, a victory over death, grace, life, spirit, pardon for our own iniquities when we repent of them, and promise of everlasting glory. Amen.

This ends Taylor's argument against a seventeenth-century concept of "original sin" held by most Presbyterians and many Anglicans. On the grounds of right reason (which his whole education inured him to) and "the liberty of prophesying" (which entailed a verse-by-verse rational exegesis of Romans 5–9), and the tradition of the Christian church before Augustine, Taylor built his argument. That his view of the problem is true answers the superficial objection that it is new, for that a thing is new is nothing against it so long as it is true. And, as a matter of fact, Taylor's views are not new. Even if Taylor's views were true, what is the necessity, cries Bishop Duppa, of disturbing the ecclesiastical peace? Answer: Truth is preferable to peace any day, especially the truth of God to the peace of man. Next, Taylor's view of original sin allows man to lead a better life. It can prepare him for repentance and so forgiveness; it does away with the excesses of spiritual pride and antinomianism which predestinarianism often brings in its train. Finally, after it is true, after it is ethically useful, it is more religious in restoring the honor of God which the doctrine of reprobation takes way from him. The polemic on original sin against the Reprobationists was one of Taylor's own choosing, against formidable opponents, and conducted at the most inopportune moment in England's church history and at a time when Taylor himself could lose his own liberty and even his life for it.

In the face of almost total agreement between Taylor and most twentieth-century biblical scholars, one might wonder what all the fuss about "total depravity" was for. Let us remember that it was in 1655, in the heat of ecclesiastical and political battle, that this usually gentle and modest scholar raised a banner emblazoned with a legend so extraordinary that it deserves capital letters:

THIS GORDIAN KNOT I HAVE NOW UNTIED, AS ALEXANDER DID,
BY DESTROYING IT AND CUTTING IT ALL IN PIECES.[4]

Apparently he had cut it so well that he brought down upon his head not only the Presbyterians and Independents but also most of the few Anglican bishops left in England by 1659 who still represented the apostolic succession. At the time of the reconstitution of the Anglican church, Taylor was famous enough to be made a bishop, but Charles II was advised to keep this dangerous thinker far away, in Ireland. As Bishop of Down and Connor, broken and lonely, Jeremy Taylor died in 1667, "a divine who once wore a mitre, and is now a little heap of dust."[5]

12   Browne's
"Letter to a Friend"

Early editors thought that Browne wrote *A Letter to a Friend* in
1672, near the end of his life. I believe it was first composed in
1656. To those of us who care this makes quite a difference, like
being persuaded that Shakespeare wrote *The Tempest* in 1596 instead of in 1612.

A Letter to a Friend concerns the death from tuberculosis of a
young man intimately known to an absent friend of the author.
Thus it performs two distinct functions, which requires its two
apparently separate parts: the attending physician describes how
the patient died, and takes this opportunity to advise his friend
how best to live. The style differs from that of Browne's ordinary
correspondence. Combining the clinical facts of a coroner's report
with a haunting view of our mortality, the main portion of the
letter shows evidence of being artistically composed and even
polished.

It was not published during the author's life but first given to
the world in 1690 by Dr. Edward Browne, Sir Thomas's distinguished medical son and literary executor. It appeared again in the
1712 *Posthumous Works*. Greenhill, Browne's nineteenth-century
editor, asserted that the *Letter* was written in 1672.[1] Walter Pater,

From my work on Sir Thomas Browne I have chosen to rewrite this essay
because it combines literary analysis with historical detective work. Parts
of the material first appeared in *Modern Philology* 48 (1951): 157–71; other
parts in "Robert Loveday: Commonwealth Man of Letters," *Review of
English Studies* 2 (1951): 262–67; and again in my book on Browne (Ann
Arbor, 1962).

however, felt what he calls "this elfin letter" bore a close kinship
with the *Hydriotaphia* of 1658:

> In its first presentation to the public this letter was con-
> nected with Browne's "Christian Morals"; but its proper
> and sympathetic collocation would be rather with the
> "Urn-Burial," of which it is a kind of prelude, and strikes
> the keynote. He is writing in a very complex situation; to a
> friend, upon occasion of the death of a common friend.
> The deceased apparently had been little known to Browne
> himself till his recent visits, while the intimate friend to
> whom he is writing had been absent at the time; and the
> leading motive of Browne's letter is the deep impression
> he has received in his visits of a sort of physical beauty in
> the coming of death, with which he still surprises and
> moves his reader.[2]

If this impression is true, then the *Letter* was first drafted in the
1650s rather than in the 1670s. Is it a generalized account of death
by tuberculosis which Browne has decorated with the literary device of the epistle, or does it describe an actual medical case? If the
latter, who were the people involved?

The title page of its first edition, 1690, is: "A Letter to a Friend
upon the Occasion of the Death of his Intimate Friend." This
means that three persons are connected by friendship in an order
of ascending intimacy, like this:

1. Dr. Browne—Patient (least intimate),
2. Dr. Browne—Recipient (more intimate),
3. Recipient—Patient (most intimate).

I believe that the patient Browne describes was Robert Loveday,
translator of La Calprenède's *Cléopâtre;* that the friend to whom
Browne wrote was Sir John Pettus; and that since Loveday died in
1656, the *Letter* was first drafted not in 1672 but two years before
Hydriotaphia was published.

For the patient we shall have to argue that Dr. Browne was
called to the bedside of Robert Loveday, who died of consumption
in 1656, and that Loveday possessed the traits of age, family, profession, and character indicated in the *Letter*. For the recipient we
shall have to persuade our readers that Loveday had an "intimate
friend" in Sir John Pettus, that Sir John was absent at the time of
Loveday's death (hence requiring a letter), and that in 1656 Dr.

Browne knew Sir John Pettus well enough to make some of the traits of the letter, particularly the advice at the end of it, applicable to him.

Before proceeding to the evidence, one might ask why no attempt has been made heretofore to identify the patient or the recipient of the letter. A conjectural answer will help to explain the kind of support for these propositions that must be used. If the letter involved Royalists before the Restoration, there were political reasons for carefully expunging all easily identifiable signs, for Cromwell's spies were still on the watch. Again, within the famous doctor's acquaintance in the East Anglican counties and in London, there might well be social reasons for concealment in view of the frankness of the advice at the end; the more distinguished the friends, the greater suppression of identity. The most important reason for deliberate erasure of personal identity is this: to the two doctors responsible for its composition and publication the detailed description of the symptoms of a patient and the results of his autopsy, accompanied by a disquisition on his character, violates the Hippocratic oath: "What I may see or hear in the course of the treatment or even outside the treatment in regard to the life of men, which on no account one must spread abraod, I will keep to myself, holding such things shameful to be spoken about."[3]

The Lovedays were an ancient family at Chediston (sometimes spelled Cheston) in East Suffolk, two miles west of Halesworth. They were probably the leading citizens in this village of scarcely two hundred people, except when Sir John Pettus, that stormy Royalist who had married the daughter of the Lord Mayor of London, swept in and out of his "country house," a mansion called Cheston Hall. Loveday aunts, uncles, and cousins, as well as brother Anthony, dwelt nearby. Robert Loveday's employment in the early 1650s was that of secretary to Lady Clinton, wife of the earl of Clare, of Nottinghamshire. In their company he traveled up and down England, though suffering from tuberculosis.

At the outset Browne mentions the well know *spes phthisca* or inordinate hope, "the common Fallacy of consumptive Persons."[4] On his first visit the doctor told the relatives that the patient would probably not live to see the next summer. He gives his friend a historical treatise on consumption, and a description of the victim's remarkable wasting away of flesh. The emaciation had been a long-drawn-out process; in his extreme thinness he reminded Browne of Dante's grotesque *omo*, his "exuccous corpse" weighing hardly more than his coffin.

From Loveday's published letters comes the evidence that when he was forced by his illness to return home to Suffolk, he was attended by Dr. Thomas Browne of Norwich. The first to mention Loveday's letters with reference to Browne's biography was D. Lloyd Roberts in 1892.[5] Sir Geoffrey Keynes, in the first edition of his Browne bibliography, doubts that the three citations in the 1662 edition of Loveday's letters refer to Thomas Browne of Norwich. He admits, however, that there was no well known "Doctor Butler" (mentioned in the letters) then living in Norwich whom the "Dr. B" might intend. Sir Geoffrey has since corrected his oversight that in Loveday's letters there are two "Dr. B.'s."

The addressee of Letter 21 is a "Dr. B." of Nottingham whom Loveday has been consulting.[6] He gradually loses confidence in this "Dr. B." to cure his "hecticall condition." At Bath with his employers, he takes the waters "according to Dr. B's prescription for my head," but it does him little good. From various places during his travels with the earl of Clare's family Robert keeps asking his brother Anthony to give his respects to "our friends in Norfolk and Suffolk" (p. 75). In Letter 56: "If your Affaires shall call you to Norwich ... I would gladly have the opinion of Dr. B from whose advise I fancy most hopes of all" (p. 100). This could not possibly be the "Dr. B" of Nottingham whose prescriptions he has been using to no avail; and the only "Dr. B." in Norwich was Dr. Thomas Browne.

Loveday wants to come "home to Norfolk" (p. 145), and he writes to his brother: "If you have a Recipe from Dr. B. of some sovereign *lotium*, it will be gratefully welcom. I am invective against cruel interest, and do upbraid my narrow condition that will not suffer me to meet you at Norwich" (p. 186). At one critical stage he has evidently received a second-hand prognosis: "I would gladly find Doctor B. not mistaken in the situation of my malady, and I hope my experience will hereafter assure me, as now my observation begins to persuade, that there is no flaw in his judgement. I have a strong fancy that shall reap much benefit by those lotions he speaks of, and therefore when you go next to Norwich let me intreat you to take note of the ingredients from his dictates" (104, pp. 192–93). By page 206 he hopes to be allowed to come "home," for "I am resolved to consult Dr. B." "This Cough I find has lately fed upon my flesh, and carried away enough from the poor store I had to make me doubt a Consumption" (p. 267).

One letter (147, pp. 271–73), addressed to "Sir," is unusual in that it is the only letter without the recipient's initials. The style is suddenly deferential, high-toned, pious, and filled with classical allusion. To this "Sir," Loveday wrote: "How oft I have wisht for a Mercurical *Caduceus* to insomniate the *Argus-eyes* of jealous people, that I might safely steal a visit, & with it the enjoyment of your happy society." It would appear that Lady Clare would not grant her secretary a leave of absence. In a strain of forced Latinity, Loveday continues his letter with allusions to the Remora, Plato's year, and Acheloan shapes, making it almost certain that he was addressing the famous author of *Religio Medici*. When Loveday finally comes home to Cheston, Dr. Browne makes a house call.

But even if Loveday were attended by Browne, he may not have been the young man of *A Letter to a Friend*. Again from his *Letters* comes the proof that he possessed the traits of age, family, profession, and moral character indicated in Browne's *Letter to a Friend*.

That Browne's patient was a young man in his early thirties is made explicit. "Consumptive and tabid Roots sprout . . . early," the doctor tells his friend, compared with other diseases: "He conceived his Thred long, in no long course of Years, and when he had scarce out-lived the second Life of Lazarus; esteeming it enough to approach the Years of his Saviour." It is a good time to die, remarks Dr. Browne, "to leave this World about that Age when most Men think they may best enjoy it." He half-congratulates the young man on dying so willingly, leaving no progeny behind him as a vain monument. Browne's literary patient died of tuberculosis close to the age of thirty-three.

Robert Loveday died in 1656 at the age of thirty-five. Venn's catalogue of Cambridge matriculations tells us he was admitted to Peterhouse.[7] Walker's *Admissions to Peterhouse*, as of the date 20 December 1636, asserts that he was admitted at the age of fifteen.[8] This means that he was born in 1621. In "An elegy on the decease of his dearly beloved brother, Mr. Robert Loveday," appended to the 1659 *Letters*, Anthony Loveday wrote:

> But whil'st he lived here seven times five years,
> (but half man's age) for time lost no arreares,

> His industry did like a River run,
> No time allow'd to sin from Sun to Sun.

If Robert Loveday was born in 1621 and died at the age of thirty-five, he died in 1656. "Thirty-five" is close enough to Browne's reference to the age of Christ and of Lazarus's second life to strengthen one's belief that Browne's patient was Robert Loveday.[9]

Of more significance than the similarity of death by tuberculosis at a comparatively young age is that Browne's patient is a literary man, a fact the doctor attempts to hide by burying it in a negative concessive clause (which I italicise): "And this serious Person, *though no minor Wit*, left the poetry of his Epitaph unto others, either unwilling to commend himself, or to be judged by a Distich, and perhaps considering how unhappy great Poets have been in versifying their own Epitaphs; wherein Petrarcha, Dante, and Ariosto have so unhappily failed. "Loveday was so well known in literary circles that Thomas Bailey, historian of Nottinghamshire, describes him in these words: "About this time [entry for 1652] there lived, as an upper servant in the family of the Earle of Clare, at Clare Hall, (Thurland House) in Nottingham, Robert Loveday, a very extraordinary person for his station in life; being an excellent scholar, well skilled in the classics, and possessing a very ready pen. He translated the three first parts of *Cleopatra*, and wrote, besides, a volume of letters, both of which performances were in good esteem with the public and *literati* of his time."[10]

Robert Loveday's major work was the unfinished translation of La Calprenède's *Cléopâtre*, a twelve-volume romance published in its French original in 1647. Before he died, he had translated the first three parts, calling his romance *Hymen's Praeludia; or, Love's Masterpiece*. These three parts were published separately in octavos beginning in 1652, then bound together and published by R. Lowndes in 1654 with commedatory poems by R. Braithwait, James Howell, John Chapperline, J. Wright, and G. Wharton.

In 1656, under the same title and with the same frontispiece, appeared the fourth part, translated by John Coles. In his dedication to Lady Jane Cheyney, Coles pays his sad respects "to the politer pen of the since deceased Loveday." In his "To the Reader" he explains that the fourth part was begun but—"'tis my grief"—not completed "by the Elegant pen of the Ingenious Loveday."

And among the congratulatory poems by Sir Kenelm Digby and others, "J. W." [John Wright?] asserts that Loveday before his untimely death had persuaded John Coles to continue the romance. Thus Loveday is alive in a preface dated 1654 and dead in another preface of 1656—the year that coincides with his death at the age of thirty-five. In addition to the translation of only a fourth of this huge French novel which thereafter bore his name, Loveday became well known for a volume of letters which his brother Anthony collected after his death and published, in obvious imitation of James Howell's *Epistolae Ho-Elianae*. That Loveday's *Letters* were in demand for a whole generation is shown by five editions of them listed in the British Library catalogue; Samuel Johnson mentioned Loveday's *Letters* in his "Life of Pope."[11] The frontispiece of the 1659 *Letters* is the portrait of Robert made by the celebrated engraver William Faithorne, with these verses:

> Wouldst know whose Face this Figure represents;
> He was the Muses Darling, in whose Tents
> He liv'd and dyde: And on whose Shrine was writ
> Here lies the paragon of Art and wit.

Browne's patient was "no minor wit."

More specifically, the patient's literary labors in Browne's *Letter* were connected with the romance languages. French and Italian allusions are more numerous than in Browne's other compositions. Hoping to gain the advantage of a change of air by "imbibing the pure Aerial Nitre of these Parts"—meaning the air of East Anglia—the patient, Dr. Browne notes, was too late; wandering about, he found "Sardinia in Tivoli" that is, the bad air of the first in the salubrious climate of the second.[12] It was an old Italian, not an Englishman, who long ago had told Dr. Browne that most people die when the moon is leaving its meridian. Instead of saying "Great Pan is dead," for some reason Browne Italianizes the Plutarchian phrase to "The great Antonio was dead."[13] We have mentioned Browne's reference to Dante's face and to the epitaphs of Petrarch, Dante, and Ariosto.

Loveday's *Letters* tell the story of his acquiring French and Italian and of the translation of La Calprenède that brought him fame so soon before he died. The Clintons used French readily (p. 30), and at one point Loveday boasts that he knows French and has begun Italian (p. 125). He reports to Sir John Pettus such progress in these two languages that "I am encouraged to publish" (p. 128). He purchases Cotgrave's *Dictionary*. The patient and the physician shared an interest in Continental tongues, particularly French and Italian.

Finally, allowing identification of the patient, Dr. Browne includes details of his character, especially his moral purity, his chastity, in which the physician observes he seemed early to have attained "the measure of a perfect stature in Christ." Chastity was a commonplace theme (witness *Comus*), yet the parallel is striking between the emphasis Browne places on this trait in his patient and the fact that Loveday dedicated his short life to a French romance enshrining this particular virtue. Loveday was too sick to think of love, marriage, and children; but there is no repining the lack of them: "All women have yet appeared so indifferent, as the whole Sex was never able to give me a Passion" (p. 74). So much for Robert Loveday as the patient in Browne's *Letter to a Friend*.

We know from the title page that Browne is writing to a friend intimately known to the deceased. The fact of a letter argues that the friend was absent at the time of the death, and we are told: "Altho at this distance you had no early Account or Particular of his Death . . ." The friend is well acquainted with the deceased's family and would recognize the allusions to several relatives. He must also be acquainted with the dead man's literary activity and either be especially interested in French and Italian himself or familiar with the deceased's knowledge of these languages. The recipient is a nonmedical man, for Browne hints that he must be ignorant of "Plautus's sick Complexion" or the famous face of Hippocrates. In spite of his ignorance of physic, the absent friend is apparently well enough educated to appreciate Browne's learned account. He is also one who would understand Browne's strange substitution of "the great Antonio" for "the great Pan is dead." The advice at the end of the letter not only grows out of the exemplum of Browne's moral lecture but also must have been thought applicable to the absent friend. That Browne presumes to give advice at all may argue that the friend is younger than he is. Who was the recipient of Browne's *Letter*?

In the preface to his dead brother's letters, Anthony Loveday boasts of the family's friendship with a well-known figure, Sir John Pettus. To start the collection off well, he places two letters

addressed to "Sir J. P." at the very beginning and there are innumerable references throughout the book to "Sir J. P." The first
item of front matter is a letter "To my friend Mr. A. L. [Anthony
Loveday]," signed "J. Pettus" and dated 14 May 1657. In this letter
he urges Anthony to publish his dead brother's letters, though
many of them are written to Sir John himself. As for his letters
written to Loveday, Sir John wishes that he had not expressed
himself as he had on certain matters of state. Of Robert Loveday,
deceased, he says at the end: "I shall onely add this . . . that I well
knew your Brother valiant, faithful, and discreetly industrious in
all the concernments of body and mind. I was his Friend." Two
sides of a correspondence indicate that he was Loveday's "intimate Friend."

Sir John Pettus (1613–90) of Rackheath, four and a half miles
northeast of Norwich, traced his pedigree through some of the
most famous families of East Anglia. His grandfather of the same
name had bought, in 1606, Overhall Manor in Rackheath, and the
family had given three mayors and many aldermen to the city of
Norwich.[14] In 1639 Sir John had married Elizabeth, daughter of Sir
Richard Gurney, Lord Mayor of London; and as a mark of favor to
Gurney had been knighted in November 1641 by Charles I. Sir
John sent money to Charles II in France after 1649, and contributed
over twenty thousand pounds to the Royalist cause. He was
wealthy enough to make himself squire of Chediston,[15] the little
village where the Lovedays had been living since Edward I. Having depleted his estate, in 1655 Sir John Pettus asked Cromwell to
appoint him deputy governor of mines in Wales. In the same year
Sir John's wife left him and turned Roman Catholic, not without
some scandal. Their daughter Elizabeth married Samuel Sandys,
and in the Sandys family home at Ombersley in Worcestershire,
R. White's portrait of Sir John Pettus hangs today.[16]

Dr. Browne knew this notorious figure, who was eight years his
junior. Propinquity, politics, and scientific interests drew them
together. The earliest mention of the Pettus family by Browne occurs in his letter to Dugdale of 6 December 1658. Three references
to Lady Pettus and one to Sir John are preserved: bits of professional gossip that Dr. Browne often indulged in in his letters to
his medical son. The earliest of these is 1679 and the latest, which
is here quoted, is dated 14 May 1681: "Sr. J. Pettus sayth hee is
well; I have not yet seen his Lady. Sr John is fallen away in his
flesh, as it is no wonder."

Was Sir John Pettus away from home when Loveday died? Though his writing career did not begin until the 1670s, by his own account Sir John became interested in geological deposits, metallurgy, and "the spagyrick arts" as a youth during summer vacations from Cambridge spent with Sir Thomas Bendish.[17] During the Civil War, Pettus continues, he knew how helpful the royal mines in Wales were to Charles I, and so in 1650 took some responsibility for their working at the behest of the Society for the Mines Royal and executed his duties faithfully "for ten years." In 1655 he became governor of mines under the Protectorate. From these references to his duties in the mines at Wales and elsewhere, particularly after 1655, we may safely infer that he was absent from the East Anglian counties at the time of Loveday's death in 1656.

The connection with Pettus explains the puzzling play on the phrase "The great Pan is dead." In 1887 W. Aldis Wright pointed out[18] that Browne's substitution of "the great Antonio" is a reference to George Sandys's *Travels* (1615).[19] Thus it may have been a subtle compliment to Sir John Pettus's daughter's marriage into the famous Sandys family.

Finally, though parts of the advice with which Browne's *Letter* closes were used in *Christian Morals*, here the *sententiae* must be considered as being of a piece with the rest. That Browne presumes to give advice is not strange. In 1656 he was just fifty, the half-century mark, an appropriate age to give advice to a friend eight years his junior who had shown by his actions that he could use it. The first paragraphs of advice have to do with chastity: a scandal, possibly connected with sex, arose when Sir John's wife left him the year before. Browne's dead man seemed not to care for riches. How wealthy Sir John was after compounding his estates is hard to say. The evidence shows that from 1655 on he was worried about money matters and could use just such advice contained in the next few paragraphs on proper attitudes toward wealth. The third group is based on the principle of *noblesse oblige*. Follow the proper ends, Browne says; don't go after applause and worldly fame. Be content to rest "in the soft showers of Providence." After giving generously to the Royalist cause, Sir John accepted from Cromwell the governorship of the mines, apparently changing sides without a qualm. All his life Sir John basked in publicity; "Rest not in an Ovation," Browne pleads. The physician calls upon his friend, apparently a man of hot temper, to calm down: "Let not thine own depravity, or the torrent of vitious

Times [The Protectorate?] carry theee into desparate Enormities in Opinions, Manners, or Actions." Did Dr. Browne, while at Loveday's house, read Sir John Pettus's letters to the patient, letters which Sir John himself confessed were politically indiscreet, written by a Royalist when Cromwell was ruler? Finally, Browne concluded, as your intimate friend died young, think of your own chances of longevity; do not act as if you owned the right to live.

These parallels between Browne's *Letter* and Loveday and between the *Letter* and Sir John Pettus cannot be weighed independently, but only within the triple relationship demanded by the *Letter* itself. Let us hope, to use Browne's ending words in our own context, that we have made "an happy Conformity, and close Apprehension of it."

Sir Thomas Browne died in 1682 and left his literary remains with his son Dr. Edward Browne. Why didn't Edward publish the letter, as he did other pieces written by his father, any time between his father's death and 1690? Why in 1690? The earliest opportunity to publish *A Letter to a Friend* when no living person could be embarrassed by it was 1690, for that was the year in which Sir John Pettus died.

The presence of parallel passages in the commonplace books and a close comparison with the shorter version in Ms. Sloan 1682 suggest that Browne had worked the letter over considerably.

It has been thought by some[20] that the shorter version is the earlier and original *Letter to a Friend*, but I think it is the end product of a twenty-year effort to write "plain," to pare down, to eliminate fancy metaphors and recondite allusions. Bishop Sprat's famous 1667 call for a scientific plain style may well have been a challenge to a writer like Browne, a scientist with a penchant for rich prose. R. F. Jones has demonstrated how during approximately the same years Glanvill, in the 1676 version of *The Vanity of Dogmatizing*, changed his style from what it had been in 1661. A single brief passage must suffice:[21]

A (1661)	*B* (1676)
But this is so largely prosecuted by that wonder of men, the Great Des-Cartes, and is a Truth that shines so clear in the Eyes of all considering men; that to goe about industriously to prove it, were to light a candle to seek the sun.	Upon which position all the Philosophy of Des-Cartes stands: And it is so clear, and so acknowledged a Truth, among all considering Men, that I need not stay to prove it.

What actually happened to Glanvill's style between 1661 and 1676 may very well, under the pressure among Englishmen of scientific bent, have happened to Browne's *Letter* between its initial composition in 1656 and his death in 1682. In *A* below we have the beginning of the second paragraph of the *Letter* in the present ornate dress we love; in *B* we have the same passage subtly simplified as it exists in Ms. Sloan 1682:

A	*B*
Altho at this distance you had no early Account or Particular of his Death, yet your Affections may cease to wonder that you had not some secret Sense or Intimation thereof by Dreams, thoughtful Whisperings, Mercurisms, Airy Nuncio's, or sympathetical Insinuations, which many seem to have had at the Death of their deceased Friends.	Though at this distance you had no particular information of his death yet your affection may cease to wonder you had not some sense or intimation thereof by dreames, visions, sympathetical communications or thoughtful whisperings which diuers seeme to haue had at the death of their dearest friends.

Fortunately for every one, the version of the *Letter* on the left with evidences of correction within it, was the version Dr. Edward Browne published in 1690. I believe it was begun in 1656, in time closer to *Urn Burial* than to the end of Browne's life.[22]

Thus it formed a kind of directive for that immortal descant on man's mortality which, with its companion piece *The Garden of Cyrus*, marks the apex in the literary development of Sir Thomas Browne.

13   Putting Taylor's Words
        to His Music

A few titles of works about Jeremy Taylor will show us how he should not be read. In 1845, "B. S. Esq., Barrister at Law" published in London *The Beauties of Jeremy Taylor: Selected from All His Devotional Writings and Sermons, with a Biographical Notice, and a Critical Examination of His Genius and Style.* But there is no biography, and the criticism consists of quoting bits from the *Quarterly Review* of 1809 and the *Edinburgh Review* of 1811 like "The piety of Taylor was adorned with the fervor of genius," or "We will venture to assert that there is in any one of the prose folios of Jeremy Taylor more fine fancy and original imagery, more brilliant conceptions and glowing expressions, more new figures and new applications of old figures; more in short of the body and soul of poetry than in all the odes and the epics that have since been produced in Europe." Pieces of him were put to practical use, as in *A Book of Family Prayers: Compiled Chiefly from the Devotions of Jeremy Taylor* by C. W. Cox (London, 1862); or *Jeremy Taylor: Brief Passages from His Writings* (London, 1882). What purports to be *The Life of Bp. Taylor* by John Wheeldon (London, 1793) consists of selections from Rust's famous funeral sermon interspersed with selections from Taylor's own prose. "This was my motive," Wheeldon says in his preface, "and was it not a pleasing one? for giving these fine pieces in miniature to the world: not having

---

I got the idea for this essay when I was working on Jeremy Taylor in the late 1960s. It has never been published.

dared to alter or retouch one original feature, but purely to revive their faded graces by the polish of a New Edition."

Possibly from perusing such nineteenth-century anthologies of Taylor's "gems" Matthew Arnold helped to promote the opposition between the kind of prose Taylor wrote and good thinking. In "The Literary Influence of the Academies" (1865) he said that England has the energy and the genius to produce the poetry of a Shakespeare but no such power as that of France in prose. Hence Newman is right, Arnold continues, in using the term "note" to describe certain English prose as having "the note of sanctity" or "the note of antiquity." Of Taylor, then, Arnold concludes that he, with Burke, possesses "the note of provinciality." He quotes "So have I seen a river" from Taylor's sermon at the funeral of Lady Carberry (which probably reminded Arnold of the *oraisons funèbres* of Bossuet), and sets beside it the intellectual power of the great French orator. Burke and Taylor are "at too great a distance from the centre of good taste," he wrote. Both are rich, imaginative, but provincial; in their prose they seldom reach that high level of intelligence called 'classical.'"

We call "unclassical" the reading of works by parts rather than by wholes. But it is also a common weakness in all of us to invite enchantment instead of challenge, to wake up during a sermon or lecture at the concrete parable or example and forget the general truth it was intended merely to illustrate. Jeremy Taylor's works fill ten volumes of great sermons, an important contribution to the history of religious toleration, well-pressed argument, and the two most popular books of devotion in our language. Who reads him? Mention his name to the average educated man and he will look into the near distance and say, "Oh yes, so have I seen a lark." Taylor's victimization by the anthologist gave birth to the quip that some one should put words to Jeremy Taylor's music.

The opponents of what came to be called the "florid" pulpit style referred to the kind of anthologized Homeric similes we have been describing as "so-have-I seen's." From an analysis of three famous "gems" we might discover just what Taylor was really accomplishing. All three appear in L. P. Smith's *The Golden Grove*, and all three reappear in a section called "Gems of Pulpit Rhetoric" in an otherwise excellent college and university textbook of English literature.

The first, naturally, is "For so have I seen a lark rising from his bed of grass and soaring upwards." The fifth sermon of *Twenty-five Sermons* (1653), from which this comes, is the central sermon in a trio entitled "The Return of Prayers; or, The conditions of a Prevailing Prayer." The trio is based on John 9:31—"Now we know that God heareth not sinners: but if any man be a worshipper of God, and doeth his will, him he heareth." The first sermon takes up the first great condition for a prevailing prayer—a pure heart; otherwise, one cannot communicate with God. After we are sanctified by repentance (first sermon), then we must condition ourselves to become fervent in prayer (the present sermon). Our prayers are often frustrated by emotions quite foreign to prayer. What happened to Claudius's prayer in *Hamlet,* and wherefore could not Macbeth say, "Amen"?

The greatest hindrance to prayer is anger, "a violent storm in the spirit of him that prays." Taylor dwells on anger, the enemy of love, "a perfect alienation of the mind from prayer." Anger in the climate of prayer becomes a human emotional storm, "contrary to that attention which presents our prayers in a right line to God." Concentrating on this adverse condition of prevailing prayer, then, Taylor writes:

> For so have I seen a lark rising from his bed of grass, and soaring upwards, singing as he rises, and hopes to get to heaven, and climb above the clouds; but the poor bird was beaten back with the loud sighings of an eastern wind, and his motion made irregular and unconstant, descending more at every breath of the tempest, than it could recover by the libration and frequent weighing of his wings; till the little creature was forced to sit down and pant, and stay till the storm was over; and then it made a prosperous flight, and did rise and sing, as if it had learned music and motion from an Angel as he passed sometimes through the air about his ministries here below: so is the prayer of a good man. [*Works,* ed. Heber-Eden, 4:61–62]

Alone it is a beautiful passage of oppositions in imagery and rhythm between the tiny will of man to ascend and the tremendous forces that press him back to earth. Taylor does not tell us that we should avoid anger; only that it is futile to try to pray while we are in its grip. The word "passion," as the opposite of "action," means something beyond our immediate control; hence the effect of anger, an impersonal force of nature, is expressed in the passive voice: "the poor bird *was beaten back*," "the little creature *was forced* to sit down and pant." The words rise with the will, but grow heavier as the lark's wings falter against the storm, until they come to a complete stop with the almost dead-weight sound of "libration," "weighing of his wings," and the trochee at the end of "stay till the storm was over." Then the sentence recovers the light "s," "f," and "p" sounds of the beginning, as well as the iambs of "and climb above the clouds." Thus, like the lark and the good man in prayer who withstands the storm of anger, or waits till it is over, the prose both rises and sings.

A similar "gem" is "For so have I seen a busy flame" from the twenty-sixth sermon of the 1651 volume of *Twenty-seven Sermons*. The important concept here is the intervening of apparent accident which men take to be fortuitous but which is the merciful hand of God that saves man from himself. Again the middle of three sermons, this one shares its title with the others: "The Miracles of the Divine Mercy" drawn from Psalm 86:5—"For thou, Lord, art good, and ready to forgive; and plenteous in mercy unto all them that call upon thee." The first sermon argues that God by representing himself as Father secures us from the hostilities of nature by his greatest tie, an unalterable and essential kindness. The next sermon recounts how he makes provisions for all our necessities, which he himself has made. He provides for our sustenance in the fruits and grain; in the very herbs of the field he gives us every medicine for the relief of our diseases. If these are his mercies for our physical life, think of the provision he makes for our life of the spirit, if, that is, we live according to the principles of his justice and mercy. So there are two channels of mercy, one on earth and the other in heaven, which double upon one another; or, to change the metaphor, when my defects of loneliness are corrected by a friend, the "two torches do not divide but increase the flame" (4:652). Thus, "when my flame hath kindled . . . [my friend's] lamp, we unite the glories, and make them radiant, like the golden candlesticks that burn before the throne of God." God unites the flames of love. But the flames of lust he stops—if we deserve the miracle of his intervention:

> For so have I seen a busy flame sitting upon a sullen coal, turn its point to all the angles and portions of its

neighbourhood, and reach at a heap of prepared straw, which like a bold temptation called it to a restless motion and activity; but either it was at too big a distance, or a gentle breath from heaven diverted the sphere and the ray of fire to the other side, and so prevented the violence of the burning; till the flame expired in a weak consumption, and died, turning into smoke and the coolness of death and the harmlessness of a cinder. And when a man's desires are winged with sails and a lusty wind of passion, and pass on in a smooth channel of opportunity, God oftentimes hinders the lust and impatient desire from passing on to its port and entering into action, by a sudden thought, by a little remembrance of a word, by a fancy, by the sudden disability, by unreasonable and unlikely fears, by the sudden intervening of company, by the very weariness of the passion, by curiosity, by want of health, by the too great violence of the desire, bursting itself with its fulness into dissolution and a remiss easiness, by a sentence of scripture, by the reverence of a good man, or else by the proper interventions of the Spirit of grace, chastising the crime, and representing its appendent mischiefs and its constituent disorder and irregularity; and after all this the very anguish and trouble of being defeated in the purpose hath rolled itself into so much uneasiness and unquiet reflections, that the man is grown ashamed, and vexed into more sober counsels. [4:653–54]

How many times have we been saved from our own bent for destruction and called ourselves lucky? Luck is accident whereas these effects are God's mercy, which does not want us to destroy his creation. The "busy flame" and "man's desire" are equally forward, stopping at nothing in the very sounds and heaped-up words in the sentence; until the providential prevention comes, in even greater "numerosity," to thwart both the flame and the evil intent. There is irony and sexual innuendo in the shift of image from fire to sea. The combination of the straw and the "shore-leave" harbor, both destructive opportunities, reminds one of another port in T. S. Eliot's use of Saint Augustine's "To Carthage then I came, burning, burning, burning." The coal merely reaches for a combustible something nearby, whereas the man arduously seeks his opportunity to "burn." But though he may find *three* (let us say) means of attaining that goal, God will place *twenty* obstacles in his way. This group of three sermons argues that it is easy to call that which happens to suit us God's providence; it is more truly God's great mercy that goes directly counter to what we mistakenly most desire. In the middle of the three sermons comes "For so have I seen a busy flame . . ." (which for some inexplicable reason did not set the house on fire).

A final example is: "So have I seen a fair structure begun with art and care" from the sermon 13 in *Twenty-five Sermons*, 1653. This too is the central of a trio of sermons, entitled "Of Lukewarmness and Zeal; or, Spiritual Fervour", based on Jeremiah 48:10—"Cursed be he that doeth the work of the Lord deceitfully." In the first sermon Taylor sets up a dichotomy between a description of this life and a projection of the other of "heavenly spirit." Between them is a third, the kingdom of grace wrought in us by God through Jesus Christ. What, then, is our duty? A double one: to serve God with all our heart and mind, that is, *wholly;* and to carry out that service with all the earnestness and intensity our affections can summon. "As our duty must be whole," Taylor begins the second sermon, "so it must be fervent" (4:154), and again he sets forth the doctrine in images of fire. God expects from us "warmth," "holy fire"; we must "enkindle the wood upon the altar"; our religion must "move upon wheels of fire"; God's breath is "fanned by the wings of the Holy Dove," and our duty therefore is to "encourage His fires" (4:156 ff.). To be fervent without but cold within is the easiest, the Laodicean hypocrisy. Such lukewarmness, rather than divine heat, is imprudent in that it never wins the goal, and it also invites a greater evil to follow. Were the second evil to come upon us with dramatic fanfare, we would avoid it. But it always comes like slow decay, a "slackened revolution" that gradually wears away the good which we had already erected and which tempted us by its fairness into a false security:

> So have I seen a fair structure begun with art and care, and raised to half its stature, and then it stood still by the misfortune or negligence of the owner, and the rain descended and dwelt in its joints, and supplanted the contexture of its pillars, and having stood a while like the antiquated temple of a deceased oracle, it fell into a hasty age, and sunk upon its knees, and so descended into ruin: so is the imperfect, unfinished spirit of man; it lays the foundation of a holy resolution, and strengthens it with vows and arts of prosecution, it raises up the walls, sacraments and prayers, reading and holy ordinances; and holy

> actions begin with a slow motion, and the building stays,
> and the spirit is weary, and the soul is naked, and exposed
> to temptation; and in the days of storm takes in everything
> that can do it mischief; and it is faint and sick, listless and
> tired, and it stands till its own weight wearies the founda-
> tion, and then declines to death and disorder, being so
> much the worse because it hath not only returned to its
> first follies, but hath superadded unthankfulness and
> carelessness, a positive neglect and a despite of holy
> things, a setting a low price to the things of God, laziness
> and wretchlessness: all which are evils superadded to the
> first state of coldness, whither he is with all these loads
> and circumstances of death easily revolved. [4:156–57]

This final "gem" connects a sermon on the whole duty of man
toward God and a sermon on the degrees of our zeal; it preaches
fervency in the face of a human temptation to slacken. The slack-
ening is borne in upon us, after the mid-break in Taylor's
sentence—"and it is faint and sick"—by nine or ten more periods
that by their very weight at the end of the sentence gradually
reduce the splendid facade to a heap of rubble—like the tower in
Wordsworth's sonnet on "Mutability." But the cause is not "the
unimaginable touch of time." Rather, something there is in
human nature that allows a lawnmower, a car, a farmer's corn-
planter, a house, a marriage, or a holy life to fall to pieces; and it
falls to pieces so slowly that we rarely blame ourselves for neglect.

Jeremy Taylor's so-called "gems," therefore are "provincial"
only as someone like Matthew Arnold separates them from the
milieu in which they are set. It is not surprising that each anthologized bit I happened to select here is central in a central
sermon of three, each trilogy based on a single theme. Metaphors
within arguments, they function as all metaphors function, to create
epistemic relationships: between the speaker and the hearer, the
abstract and the concrete, what has gone before and what comes
after, what is being said and the way of its saying. This is how
style should be read, and Logan Pearsall Smith, among others,
knew it: "For a great prose," he once wrote of Donne's sermons,
"needs a great subject matter, needs great themes and a high
spectacular vision, a solemn and steadfast conception of life and
meaning."

14   Vultures, Chinese Land-Ships, and Milton's "Paradise of Fools"

As when a Vultur on *Imaus* bred,   (431)
Whose snowy ridge the roving *Tartar* bounds,
Dislodging from a Region scarce of prey
To gorge the flesh of Lambs or yeanling Kids
On Hills where Flocks are fed, flies toward the
     Springs   (435)
Of *Ganges* or Hydaspes, Indian streams;
But in his way lights on the barren Plains
Of *Sericana*, where *Chineses* drive
With Sails and Wind thir cany Waggons light:
So on this windy Sea of Land, the Fiend
Walk'd up and down alone bent on his prey,   (440)
     Alone, . . .

This simile in book 3 of *Paradise Lost* introduces the "Paradise of Fools," a passage that has graveled readers and scholars by its shocking anti-Catholicism. Verity, for instance, in 1910 said that the "almost burleque satire of the passage seems scarce in keeping with the dignity of an epic."[1] Professor Hughes asserts that here Milton "wrote an invective of the Roman Church as unexpected as his attack upon the venal clergy in *Lycidas*."[2] Witty and almost scabrous as the whole passage of sixty-six lines is, has Milton the Puritan allowed his anti-Catholic bias to get in the way of his art?

This essay in persuasion combines two earlier articles: "A Justification of Milton's 'Paradise of Fools,'" *ELH* 21 (1954): 107–13; and "Milton, Mendoza, and the Chinese Land-ship." *MLN* 69 (1954), 404–7. Bits may appear in my brief note for *The Milton Encyclopedia*.

Although Milton had been almost as bitter about the prelates and presbyters, still the anti-Catholic invective is there.

It appears to be a digression in the goliardiac tradition, or that of Sebastian Brandt's *Das Narrenschiff*, translated into English by Alexander Barclay in 1509 as *The Ship of Fools*. Parallels have been found to *Orlando Furioso* (cf. line 459) and to Burton's *Anatomy of Melancholy* (3. 4). Some scholars trace its source to the myth of Er in Plato's *Republic* (10. 614), or to the description in the *Phaedo* of souls who because they fail to nurture themselves on reason will eventually "be scattered and blown away by the winds."

Whatever the ancient literary sources may be, some more recent European history lies behind the passage. After the Spanish Armada and the Gunpowder Plot, Roman Catholics, particularly the Jesuits, were looked upon by almost every Englishman as the archenemy. It is little realized, however, that part of Milton's anti-Roman invective here is contained in the apparently innocent allusion to the Chinese custom of traveling across their plains in bamboo wagons driven by wind power (lines 437–39). Allan Gilbert[3] has pointed out that the primary source of Milton's knowledge of the Chinese land-ship was a Spanish friar from Toledo, Juan Gonzalez de Mendoza, whose account of it was published in 1585.

Mendoza's book was translated into English in 1588 by Robert Parke as *The Historie of the Great and Mighty Kingdome of China, and the Situation Thereof; Together with the Great Riches, Huge Cities, Politicke Government, and Rare Inventions in the Same*.[4] The translator in his long preface warns his readers not to be taken in by anything coming from a Roman Catholic source; nevertheless among the "rare inventions" he gives great prominence to the Chinese land-ship:

> They are great inventers of things, that though they have amongst them many coches and waggons that goe with sailes, and made with such industrie and policie that they do governe them with great ease: this is crediblie informed by many that have seene it: besides that, there be many in the Indies and in Portugall, that have seene them painted upon clothes, and on their earthen vessell that is brought from thence to be solde: so that is a signe that their painting hath some foundation.[5]

Depictions of land-ships on Chinse silk screens and porcelains seemed to be enough for Robert Parke.

Simon Stevin (1558–1620), the great Dutch expert in hydro-statics, however, constructed about the year 1600, from Mendoza's description, two sailing chariots, one large and one small.[6] He invited as guests for a trial spin Mendoza himself, then a prisoner of war at the Hague, Prince Maurice of Nassau, and Hugo Grotius, then a youth of seventeen, and many others. The ships traveled north on the sand flats from Scheveningen to Pettin at the in-credible speed of thirty to thirty-five miles an hour. Grotius, who rode in the larger ship with twenty-seven other passengers, was so enthusiastic that he described the experience in his *Parallelon Rerum-publicarum*, as well as in several Latin poems.[7] Meanwhile, Jan Huyghen van Linschoten had published a description, also based on Mendoza, in *Itinario* (1596).[8] De Gheyn's famous print of Stevin's land-chariots, splendidly rigged, spread throughout Europe the Dutch engineer's, rather than the actual Chinese, con-ception of what a Chinese wind-wagon looked like. In his *Thea-trum Orbis Terrarum*, Ortelius adorned his map of China with four very handsome Dutch-Chinese land-ships,[9] and there are allusions to the device in Hakluyt's *Voyages*, Heylin's Cosmog-raphie, and Ben Jonson's *News from the New World*.

Made a bit more respectable by the ingenious and Protestant Dutch, still the Chinese land-ship began with the description by just such a Catholic priest as Milton derides in "Paradise of Fools." Could he be making a pun on Mendoza and the Latin word for prevarication?

Milton's vulture simile coincides with the monstrous Satan's reaching a midpoint in his journey from Hell to Earth. High on the top of our solar universse he pauses to contemplate his mission. Above him the chain links our huge ball to the ramparts of Heaven. About its foot lies a dark, wild waste, buffeted by the tempests of Chaos.

Although Gilbert has identified the names in the geography of this vulture, the homology of the vulture and Satan derives sig-nificance from the juncture of the plot. The vulture is a bird of prey, and Satan, a wicked winged fiend, is "bent on his prey," who like "yeanling kids" (just born) are unaware of their danger. Though this vulture was bred on Imaus, the mountain range of

snow that stretches, on seventeenth-century maps, across Asia
from Afghanistan up to the Arctic, it intends to fly on to India,
more fertile ground. Satan is on his way to Eden, and even the two
Indian rivers suggest another fertile valley nestling between two
rivers, the Tigris and Euphrates. As the snowy region of Imaus is
the point of egress for the vulture, so Satan had crossed that part of
Hell which is not fire but *ice:*

> Beyond this flood a frozen Continent
> Lies dark and wild, beat with perpetual storms
> Of whirlwind and dire Hail, which on firm land
> Thaws not, but gathers heap, and ruin seems
> Of Ancient pile; all else deep snow and ice.
>
> [2. 587–91]

What's more, this "snowy ridge" of Imaus was supposed to
"bound" the "roving Tartar" (432). Geographically it did "bound"
Tartary in the 1636 edition of Mercator's *Atlas*. And Tartaria would
remind Milton of Tartarus, the infernal regions of ancient Greek
and Roman mythology. But Imaus did not keep the Tartars from
"roving"; they came out of their fastness to devastate Asia and
eastern Europe—even as this vulture has emerged from frozen
Imaus and Satan has broken out of the ice of Hell.

Though Satan is alone now, if cause and effect still work, he will
not be alone after he has completed his nefarious mission. He will
populate this very place, which has been cursed, as it were by his
visit:

> Alone, for other Creature in this place   (442)
> Living or lifeless to be found was none,
> None yet, but store hereafter from the earth
> Up hither like Aereal vapours flew
> Of all things transitorie and vain, when Sin   (445)
> With vanity had filld the works of men:
> Both all things vain, and all who in vain things
> Built thir fond hopes of Glorie or lasting fame,
> Or happiness in this or th' other life;   (450)
> All who have thir reward on Earth, the fruits
> Of painful Superstition and blind Zeal,
> Naught seeking but the praise of men, here find
> Fit retribution, emptie as thir deeds;
> All th' unaccomplisht works of Natures hand,   (455)
> Abortive, monstrous, or unkindly mixt,

Dissolvd on earth, fleet hither, and in vain,
Till final dissolution, wander here,
Not in the neighbouring Moon, as some have dreamd;
Those argent Fields more likely habitants,
Translated Saints, or middle Spirits hold
Betwixt th' Angelical and Human kinde:
Hither of ill-joyned Sons and Daughters born
First from the ancient World those Giants came
With many a vain exploit, though then renownd: (465)
The builders next of *Babel* on the Plain
Of *Sennaar*, and still with vaine designe
New *Babels*, had they wherewithall, would build:
Others came single; hee who to be deemd
A God, leap'd fondly into Ætna flames,
Empedocles, and hee who to enjoy
Plato's Elysium, leap'd into the Sea,
Cleombrotus, and many more too long,
Embryo's and Idiots, Eremits and Friars
White, Black, and Grey, with all thir trumperie.   (475)
Here Pilgrims roam, that stray'd so farr to seek
In *Golgotha* him dead, who lives in Heav'n;
And they who to be sure of Paradise
Dying put on the weeds of *Dominic*,
Or in *Franciscan* think to pass disguis'd;   (480)
They pass the Planets seven, and pass the fixt,
And that Crystalline Sphear whose ballance weighs
The Trepidation talkt, and that first mov'd;
And now Saint *Peter* at Heav'ns Wicket seems
To wait them with his Keys, and now at foot   (485)
Of Heav'ns ascent they lift thir Feet, when loe
A violent cross wind from either Coast
Blows them transverse ten thousand Leagues awry
Into the devious Air; then might ye see
Cowles, Hoods and Habits with thir wearers tost   (490)
And flutterd into Raggs, then Reliques, Beads,
Indulgences, Dispenses, Pardons, Bulls
The sport of Winds: al these upwhirld aloft
Fly o'er the backside of the World farr off
Into a *Limbo* large and broad, since calld   (495)
The Paradise of Fools, to few unknown
Long after, now unpeople'd, and untrod; . . .

It is pride and its concomitant falsehood and deceit that Milton
scores. Since the proud priests in this "Pardise of Fools" (often

called the "Limbo of Vanities") disguise themselves in billowy
gowns that catch the adverse winds, Milton hints in his simile that
a wagon equipped with sails is not what it seems to be. The
inhabitants traverse a "windy sea of land" (line 440) at the top of
our universe, something like the billowy surface we saw on our
television screens as the first humans stepped onto the moon.

The satirical grotesquerie of the images here is in keeping with a
technique that may be thought of as the opposite of the movie
flashback. It carries us forward imaginatively to those who, like
Satan, also pause on a journey from Earth up to this wind-swept
plain. In the motley crowd a number of Catholic priests and friars
are blown about amidst their relics, indulgences, cowls, and habits.
A grand irony and seething anger appropriately attend this his-
torica moment in the birth of human pride, as Satan projects his
foul mission from the top of our world. Here, far short of Heaven,
the future victims of his crime will inhabit their Paradise of Fools
on the very spot where the fiend decides to go on rather than to go
back.

For, to the blustery place where Satan just now is wandering
alone, Sin and Death, his hideous relatives, anchor the nearer
end of the causeway they build from Hell, by their punning "Art
pontifical":

> Now have they brought the work by wondrous Art
> Pontifical, a ridge of pendent Rock
> Over the vext Abyss, following the track
> Of *Satan*, to the selfsame place where hee
> First lighted from his Wing, and landed safe
> From out of *Chaos* to the outside bare
> Of this round World: . . .
>
> [10. 312–18]

It seems to be no accident, then, that in book 10, to anticipate this
rendezvous, Milton has Death (the wages of Sin) smell out his
future victims like a vulture—not one vulture, this time, but

> As when a flock   (450)
> Of ravenous Fowl, though many a League remote,
> Against the day of Battle, to a Field
> Where Armies lie encampt, come flying lur'd
> With scent of living Carcasses design'd
> For death, the following day, in bloody fight.   (455)

>So scented the grim Feature, and upturn'd
>His Nostril wide into the murky Air,
>Sagacious of his Quarry from so far. . . .
>
>[10. 273–81]

From the long description of the paradise of future fools two sets of key images emerge. One set is *hypocrisy, disguise, vanity,* and *being tossed to and fro by winds.* The other is *miscegenation, embryos, giants,* and *monstrous births.*

The central sin is pride. Vanity, its outward effect, is a kind of disguise. Satan in Hell was a superbly proud creature. Out of Hell, to bring sin into the world, he stoops to guile, pretense, and a series of disguises. He disguises himself as a good cherub to ask Uriel the way to Earth. Then he disguises himself, descendingly, as a cormorant, a toad, and finally a serpent. After hinting that the Chinese in the simile *disguise* their wagons as boats Milton shows some people in Limbo dressed up in religious gowns that billow like sails as they catch the strong transverse winds (487). Blown every which way by what, to Milton in the seventeenth century and even to sound present-day Catholic opinion, are false winds of doctrine, the poor souls "here find fit retribution, empty as their deeds" (454). For "Indulgences, Dispenses, Pardons, Bulls" in the politics of the church in Reformation times rested on false doctrine—the problem is to discern it. Ever since writing *Comus,* in which the devil is disguised as a charming fellow, Milton had underscored the main trouble with sin: you can't always see it for what it is. Through guile the devil begets evil on good. And in the next book (4. 121–22), as Satan lands in Eden, Milton tells us that he "was the first / That practic'd falsehood under saintly show"—being a forerunner of Chaucer's Pardoner and Spenser's Archimago.

In addition to vanity, bluster, and disguise, there is another note—that of miscegenation or the "fruit" of misalliance. By anticipation this bitter fruit follows the plucking of that other fruit in Eden. Into this Limbo are blown all those things and people that are "abortive, monstrous, or unkindly mixed" (456), where "unkindly" means "unnaturally" or not according to "kind." Here the history of "ill-joined sons and daughters" (463) begins with the giants of ancient times, comes through the builders of the tower of Babel, includes Empedocles and Cleombrotus (both of whom vainly hoped to reach Heaven sans grace, through suicide), and ends with the Dominicans, Franciscans, and Carmelites of Milton's own day. Through the concept of miscegenation Milton echoes here the monstrous birth of Sin and Death, whom Satan, on his way to this spot, had just met at the gates of Hell. Sin issued full-blown like Minerva, with some poetic justice, out of the head of Satan. Upon this female creature Satan incestuously begot Death. In turn Death raped his mother (Satan's daughter and mistress) and begot on her a litter of yelping monsters. It is a horrendous myth for the involution of evil—evil which is a willful rebellion against natural law.

Hence the giants of line 464 are connected by Milton's imagination with Hesiod's war between the wisdom of the gods and brutishness of the titans, with the biblical giants of Anakim the chosen of God had to overthrow, with the giants of Cornwall which his reading in Geoffrey of Monmouth for his *History of Britain* and which his fondness for Arthurian legend had lodged in his poetic brain for so long. There was also the myth of Hercules vanquishing the giant Antaeus, which in *Paradise Regained* (4. 563 ff.) symbolizes Christ breaking the serpent's head. The fall of man started in Heaven with the "Earth-born" instincts of the proud angels led by Lucifer. Thus in the very first similitude of Satan in *Paradise Lost* (1. 196), Satan lies "in bulk as huge / As whom the Fables name of monstrous size, Titanian, or Earth-born, that warr'd on Jove."

The final impression one receives from the whole Limbo passage is that of monstrosity and wind, the cause and the effect of sin. For sin is caused by a violation of nature, a defection from rational norms; and its result is that the victims are themselves powerless in a storm of billowing gusts that sweep them "ten thousand leagues awry." The apparently disparate concepts of perverted sex and strong wind unite in the symbol of the vulture. In many a seventeenth-century emblem book, this ill-omened bird is depicted as a hermaphroditic female which fertilizes its eggs by sitting on high crags and allowing strong winds to blow on its tail.[10] Though Sir Thomas Browne had corrected the "vulgar error,"[11] the suggestion of the vulture's self-generation by wind powerfully expresses Milton's insistence upon the single and monstrous hatching of evil.

The Paradise of Fools is not an extraneous passage. Through

these images of wind and monstrous birth, the apparent digression is associated with book 1, with the birth of Sin and Death in 2, and with the mountain-throwing climax of Raphael's account of the war in Heaven. It also anticipates the temptation and fall in 9; immediately after the primal sin Adam and Eve wept,

> nor only Tears
> Rain'd at thir Eyes, but high Winds worse within
> Began to rise . . . and shook sore
> Thir inward State of Mind, calm region once
> And full of Peace, now toss't and turbulent;
> For Understanding rul'd not. . . .
>
> [9. 1121–27]

Finally, in its form of projected history, the passage foreshadows the last two books, which allow Adam to foresee the historical effects of his sin: the justness of his banishment through the largesse of grace. The sinners that Michael shows Adam by turning history forward are

> the product
> Of those ill-mated Marriages thou saw'st
> Where good with bad were matcht, who of themselves
> Produce prodigious births of body or mind.
> Such were the Giants, men of high renown;
>
> [11. 683–88]

Read like this, the passage is not a gratuitous blemish in an otherwise well-constructed whole. Milton justifies its inclusion and position not only by the simile of the vulture landing in China, but also by his whole plot, his cosmic setting, and his moral intention. Its anti-Catholicism, there by history, ceases to be topical as it is raised by Milton's artistry to become a symbol of pride.

As soon as the futuristic nightmare is over, he returns us to his epic soon enough. But the tone he wanted has been set for the ironically idyllic description of Paradise to follow; since the "fools" in this Limbo are the children, like us, of our first parents, free "to choose / Their place of rest, and Providence their guide."

Endings: To My Friend
Ed Burklund (1897–1964)

Ed and I first met in the early autumn of 1944 at a colleague's house for dinner, when our family was newly arrived in Ann Arbor. Things were rather formal until suddenly we realized that everyone at the table was a Democrat. Then conversation became lively and the jokes uproarious. Ed Burklund and I felt that night, as we discussed the phenomenon many times later, a peculiar bond of kinship, for we were nursed on the selfsame hill. At different colleges we had been weaned on Shelley, Keats, A. E. Housman, Thackeray, Tschaikovsky, *The Education of Henry Adams,* George Gissing, Fitzgerald's *Rubaiyat of Omar Khayyam;* we had read Santayana and our most radical support had been H. L. Mencken.

When we met again soon after, we found ourselves quoting from memory the same poems. My family affectionately called him "C. S.," because one time (and how he loved to repeat his stories) a former Japanese student had addressed a letter to "C. S. Buckland Esquire." He is still "C. S." to me of sweetest memory.

"Frank," how often he would say, "I love you. Is there anything wrong in that?" "No, C. S.," I would reply: "I love you too and that's the first time I've ever said that to a man." "Me too, godammit, that's funny, isn't it?"

A deep friendship can exist between two men who, like most of us in "the profession of English," love literature, conviviality, and gentle argument. This essay is the introduction to the memorial volume of Edwin Burklund's beautiful Michigan poems which I edited as *The Moment of Time.* This was issued privately in Ann Arbor in 1973, and the introduction is reprinted here with the kind permission of Mrs. Burkland.

C. S. was a rich human being, handsome as a viking, a great scholar (chary of publishing, though his articles on the oral interpretation of poetry are standard bibliography), and above all a poet. His Ph.D. in German literature had come much earlier than my graduate work, and he was skeptical of my approach in what was then known as "the new criticism." For hours we argued over the meaning of particular poems; he would go immediately to the core of feeling, and I would analyze the structure of the whole and the relationship of parts. In these arguments I confess to feeling intellectually superior. But I was talking all around the poem, and he knew the poem.

Our quoting poems together often took a certain pattern. "The hunched camels of the night / Trouble the bright / And stilly waters of the moon," I would start off. "Goddammit, Frank;" C. S. would interrupt, "what poet would ever use a silly word like 'stilly'? The word is 'silver.' Want to bet?" "Goddammit, C. S.," I would return, "what poet would ever use a cliché like *'silver* waters of the moon'?" Well, C. S. and Francis Thompson were right, and C. S. was always right. He was a nineteenth-century romantic poet himself, and in twenty years of quoting poems with him I never won a single bet.

Ed, as he was called by almost everyone, knew poetry. And not only English poetry, but that of almost every European language. I envied his reading Homer in Greek for the sheer pleasure of it. He could quote Vergil twenty or forty lines at a time, and Horace and Catullus. He had read all of French poetry, and Spanish, and German, and Italian, and of course his ancestral language, which was Swedish, he dearly loved. Unlike the rest of us in academia, he never felt the need of spending a sabbatical abroad; the best of Europe was on his shelves and in his head.

Ed had a gust for living such as I have rarely known. We were younger in those days and could drink more, and how we did drink. The more we drank the more flowing our memories became and the more mellifluous our voices. We drank the cheapest kinds of bourbon we could find, the more regional and bucolic the name on the label the better. For a season we thought peppermint schnapps a fine rural drink and almost made ourselves sick on it. One Saturday in two hours of listening to a football game on the radio we consumed between us a case of beer. I didn't believe it, but C. S. won that argument by carefully counting for me the twenty-four empty bottles we had rolled under the davenport. And in our cups we sang. He had a fine rich voice that could carry an air accurately. Around it I attempted to weave sometimes a whiskey tenor and at other times a tremulous baritone. Our masterpiece was the "Crusaders' Hymn," which we sang so beautifully that tears would flow down our cheeks. Being a Civil War buff he was fond of the "Battle Hymn of the Republic," especially the last stanza, sung very softly, "In the beauty of the lilies Christ was born across the sea." I taught him in Spanish "La Paloma"; but when we came to the flamenco chorus, instead of singing the real words C. S. would sing in the same rhythm "Pleased to meetcha, pleased to meetcha" with a shuffle of his feet and a huge grin on his face. Over a hundred times our lovely Spanish duet never ended except in guffaws and shaking hands all around.

"Nature I loved, and next to Nature, Art; / I warmed both hands before the fire of life, / It sinks, and . . ." C. S. loved the land and the trees and animals. On many a long summer night our two families sat on the Lake Michigan shore talking, or singing, or mostly just gazing into the deep embers of a driftwood fire and listening to the rhythm of the waves. He loved, especially at night, the great marsh near the home of his parents-in-law in Hastings, Michigan; the cut-over fields, the stream, and the woods at White Cloud in Newaygo County; and later the beautiful home, which he and his dear wife Edna restored with their own hands, in the rich natural setting of twenty-six acres in Unadilla.

He had the common touch, and could carry on a conversation with a farmer, the village storekeeper, the local parson if you please, for he had a deep sense of religion though he did not care much about church. With that old-world courtliness and instinctive kindness, he earned the affection of the two elderly spinster sisters who lived nearby. One neighbor in need of cash sold him a battered suitcase for a dollar and a half. C. S. didn't need a suitcase. The negotiations went on philosophically and charitably for three weeks, but the re-telling lasted for fifteen years. "What's the name of yer dog?" the man asked. "Sappho," replied C. S. Howdja spell it?" the man asked. "S-A-P-P-H-O," replied C. S. "Sappo," the man said, "that's a helluva name fer a dog."

Though no Swede myself, I have to have a cup of strong black coffee as soon as I get up. One morning I rose early to find C. S.

chopping wood for the iron cookstove. "The coffee will be ready in a minute," he said. "I think I'll go downtown for a cup of coffee," I said. "It'll only be a minute," he said, as, standing ten feet away, he threw a full pint of kerosene at the smouldering fire. The back bedroom under the eaves was infested with thousands of torpid wasps, and after breakfast we sucked them up one by one into the tube of the old Hoover. Each full vacuum-cleaner bag we placed in the fire would remind C. S. of some line in an Icelandic saga.

He would often quote from Banville, "Nous n'irons plus au bois, les lauriers sont coupés." All beauty put tears into his eyes, and so did the almost unendurable irony of being a "Lover of beauty in an hour." Like Shakespeare, Blake, Keats, Donne, Browne, T. S. Eliot, Frost, and every authentic poet before him, Ed was deeply aware of "the moment of time." He knew that the very fact of being born decrees that the laurel trees be cut down and that never again can we go into those woods.

Notes

Chapter Two

1. The definitive edition is edited by J. B. Leishman, *The Three Parnassus Plays* (Liverpool, 1949). All my quotations from the plays are from this edition.

2. *Historical Manuscripts Commission, Twelfth Report, Appendix,* pt. 1 (London, 1881), p. 19.

3. *The Collected Poems of Joseph Hall,* ed. A. Davenport (Liverpool, 1949), my italics.

4. Recorded by Leishman: Introduction, p. 7.

5. Alfred Hart, *Shakespeare and the Homilies* ... (Melbourne, 1934), p. 122, finds the average of 204 extant printed plays between 1590 and 1616 (excluding Jonson's) to be 2,447 lines.

6. *The Poems of John Marston,* ed. A. Davenport (Liverpool, 1961).

7. Venn, *Alumni Cantabrigiensis* (Cambridge, 1927), 4:354.

8. Arber, *Stationers' Register,* 3:677; Leishman, Introduction, pp. 44, 51, 72.

9. *Weever's Faunus and Melliflora (1600),* ed. A. Davenport (Liverpool, 1948), Introduction, p. vi.

10. *Crudities* (Glasgow, 1905), 4. 174–75.

11. *An Itinerary* (Glasgow, 1908), 4. 28, 34. In 1635 Dr. Thomas Browne deplored the uncharitableness of such national stereotypes as are contained in the verse ending, "*L'Espagnol superbe, et l'Aleman yvrongne*" (*Rel. Med.,* 2. 4).

12. See the college accounts for wine and beer, G. C. Moore, *College Plays Performed in the University of Cambridge* (Cambridge, 1923), p. 33. See also the speech by Momus already quoted about "emptying the college barrels," and the same character's "You may doe better to busy your selfe in

prouiding beere, for the shewe will be pittiful drie, pittiful drie" ("Progresse," lines 54–55).

13. The Roxburgh Club, 1873, p. 221.

14. *The Whipping of the Satyre*, ed. A. Davenport (Liverpool, 1951), p. 6.

15. Leishman, Introduction, p. 33.

16. *Whipping of the Satyre*, Introduction, pp. viii–ix.

17. Weever's *Epigrammes*, ed. R. B. McKerrow (Stratford-upon-Avon, 1911).

18. *An Itinerary*, 4. 139.

Chapter Three

1. Most Jonsonians date the play 1598, but W. David Kay, "The Shaping of Ben Jonson's Literary Career: A Reexamination of Facts and Problems," *Modern Philology*, 67 (1970), 226–27, argues well for 1597.

2. W. W. Greg, *A Bibliography of the English Printed Drama to the Restoration* (London, 1939–51), 1:417–18.

3. *The Works of Ben Jonson: In Seven Volumes…*, ed. Peter Whalley, vol. 1 (London, 1756), Preface, p. xxv.

4. Ibid., p. xxiv.

5. *The Case Is Altered, by Ben Jonson*, ed. W. E. Selin (Yale Studies in English, vol. 56, 1917), Introduction, pp. xvi–xxix.

6. My citations of *The Case Is Altered* are to the text edited by C. H. Herford and Percy Simpson, *Ben Jonson*, vol. 3 (Oxford, 1927), pp. 105–90.

7. Selin (Introduction, p. xvii) finds this parallel so important that he places it alone in his text of commentary rather than among the notes.

8. John J. Enck, *Jonson and the Comic Truth* (University of Wisconsin Press, 1957), chap. 2, which elaborates his article in *SP* 50 (1952): 195–214.

9. Enck, *Jonson*, p. 23.

10. *Palladis Tamia*, ed. Don Cameron Allen (New York, 1938), facsimile of 1598, p. 283.

11. *Works of Thomas Nashe*, ed. R. B. McKerrow, 3 (London, 1910): 220.

12. *N & Q*, 10th ser., 11 (1909): 41–42.

13. J. F. Bradley and J. Q. Adams, *The Jonson Allusion-Book* (New Haven, 1922), p. 50.

14. Cf. *Hamlet*, 4. 5. 172–73. Did Munday write a ballad, now lost, on his story of Jacques and his stolen daughter which crept into Ophelia's mad scene?

15. The dating rests on the assumption that "A.M.," editing *Belvedere*, would not choose to quote from a play which had been used to satirize him; hence the satire must have been added after *Belvedere* was published in 1600. Cf. Roscoe A. Small, *The Stage-Quarrel between Ben Jonson and the So-called Poetasters* (Breslau, 1899), p. 179; and E. K. Chambers, *The Elizabethan Stage* (Oxford, 1923), 3:357.

16. Selin, Introduction, p. xvii.

17. Herford and Simpson, 3:434 (lines 177–84).

18. Jonson characterizes his Asper as "One, whom no seruile hope of gaine, or frosty apprehension of danger, can make to be a Parasite, either in time, place, or opinion" (Herford and Simpson, 3:423).

19. Eustace Conway, *Anthony Munday and Other Essays* (New York, 1927), p. 44; and Celeste Turner, *Anthony Munday: An Elizabethan Man of Letters* (Berkeley, University of California Publications in English, vol. 2, 1928).

20. The word "untruss" was bandied about in the quarrel, the title of a popular 1586 ballad by Munday. Nashe and Dekker both use it.

21. *The Plays of John Marston,* ed. H. Harvey Wood. vol. 3 (London, 1939): 260.

22. Chambers, 2:52–53; Herford and Simpson, 9:166.

23. J. M. Nosworthy in *JEGP* 51 (1952): 61–70, argues that Henry Porter is the "other author" besides Jonson. The latest work on Jonson, Twayne's English Authors Series, no. 268, by Claude Summers and Ted-Larry Pebworth (Boston, 1979), pp. 48–49, does not question Jonson's authorship.

Chapter Four

1. In 1679 Pope Innocent XI condemned the doctrine of equivocation as "Laxismus," and thus it finds it place in that little volume popularly known as "The Index." Moral theologians of the Roman Catholic faith have since been silent about it.

2. *A Complete Collection of State Trials,* ed. T. B. Howell 2 (1816): 234.

3. *Calendar of State Papers, Domestic Series, 1603–1610* (London, 1816).

4. *I, William Shakespeare* (New York, 1938), pp. 172–202.

5. Navarrus was born in 1491 and died in Rome at the age of ninety-five in 1586. A complete edition of his works was published at Rome in 1590, and again at Venice in 1601 and 1602.

6. Navarrus cites the incident in *Humane Aures,* 22, quaest. r, from the lives of Saint Francis by Angelus de Perusio and Johannes ad Anonia.

7. No. 968 (E. 45), Laud's quarto catalogue, misc. no. 655 (Casuistry). It was transcribed and published by Jardine at London in 1851.

8. These same criteria for swearing an oath are contained in the last of the "Thirty-nine Articles" in *The Book of Common Prayer.* Does anyone know when the phrase "the whole truth" was added to our oath?

9. Cf. the beginning of *De interpretatione,* tr. E. M. Edgehill, *The Works of Aristotle* (Oxford, 1928, 1937), vol. 1, 16a.

10. Traditionally John Donne helped Bishop Morton frame his anti-Jesuitical argument, *An Exact Discovery of Romish Doctrine in the Case of Conspiracy and Rebellion,* 4 vols. (London, 1605). STC, no. 18184; cf. *DNB.*

11. *The Execution of Justice in England ... xviii. Decemb. 1583.* STC, no. 4902.

12. *The Anatomie of Popish Tyrannie* ..., p. 3.

Chapter Five

1. Quotations of Hall's *Characters* are from the edition of *Heauen and Earth and Characters of Vertues and Vices* by Rudolf Kirk (New Brunswick, N.J., 1948).

2. Beginning perhaps with the edition of Theophrastus by Sir Richard Jebb in 1870.

3. E. C. Baldwin, "The Relation of the English 'Character' to its Greek Prototype," *PMLA,* 18 (1903): 412–24. Almost all we know about the "character" lies in two books, both published by Harvard University Press in 1947: *The Theophrastan Character in England to 1642,* by Benjamin Boyce, and *A Bibliography of the Theophrastan Character in England,* by Chester Noyes Greenough. An excellent estimate of Hall's is Gerhard Muller-Schwefe (Tübingen), in *Texas Studies in Language and Literature* 14 (1972): 235–51. Cf. E. N. S. Thompson, *Literary Bypaths of the Renaissance* (New Haven, Conn., 1924) and Wendell Clausen, "The Beginnings of English Character-Writing in the Early Seventeenth Century," *Philological Quarterly* 25 (1946): 32–45.

4. *A Book of Characters* (London and New York, 1924), p. 9.

5. One of the most devastating descriptions of James's character is that by William Harris, *An Historical and Critical Account ...* 2nd ed. (London, 1772).

6. From Hall's autobiography, "Some Specialities in the Life of Joseph Hall," written in prison in 1641.

7. James VI, *Basilikon Doron,* ed. James Craigie, the Scottish Text Society, 3d ser., no. 16 (1944), p. 35.

8. Facsimile edition by W. T. Costello, S. J., and C. Keenan, S.J. (Gainesville, Florida, 1965).

9. J. Nichols, *The Progresses ... of King James the First* (London, 1828), 2:62.

10. *The Works of Bishop Joseph Hall,* ed. Philip Wynter 10 vols. (Oxford, 1863), 5:106.

11. Nichols, *The Progresses of James the First,* 4:1037, as reported by William le Neve in a letter to Sir Thomas Holland, 25 April 1625.

12. In the King James versions of Proverbs and Ecclesiastes, the words "wise" and "wisdom" occur fifty-three times; and the words "Fool," "Foolish," and "folly" more often than in all the other books of the Bible combined.

13. See Per Palme, *Triumph of Peace: A Study of the Whitehall Banqueting House, Figura,* vol. 8 (Stockholm, 1965).

14. *Proceedings of the Leeds Philosophical Society,* vol. 6 (1950).

15. See William Whallon's study of "Hebraic synonymy" in Browne's prose, *ELH*, 28 (1961), 335–52.

16. One of the many insights Leonard Tourney gives us in *Joseph Hall* (Boston: Twayne no. 250, 1979) is that Hall's "Happy Man" summarizes all the virtues because his Christian devotion sets him far above Senecan morality (chap. 3, "The Taxonomy of Morals," p. 51).

17. Mark Pattison, *Isaac Casaubon, 1559–1614* (Oxford, 1892), p. 264. In 1608, the year *Characters* was published, Archbishop Bancroft gave King James a copy of *De libertate ecclesiastica*. His Majesty "had been so delighted with it, that for many days he could talk of nothing but Casaubon" (ibid., p. 272).

Chapter Six

1. Leo Spitzer, *Classical and Christian Ideas of World Harmony*, ed. Anna G. Hatcher, Preface by René Wellek (Baltimore, Md., 1961), originally published in *Traditio* 2 (1944): 409–64; 3 (1945): 307–64.

2. Of the several studies of Johnson's famous essay on Cowley I find the least fruitful W. B. C. Watkins, *Johnson on English Poetry before 1660* (Princeton, 1936), pp. 78–84; and most fruitful Allen Tate, "Johnson on the Metaphysical Poets," *Kenyon Review* (1952).

3. Cf. G. S. Kirk and J. E. Raven, *The Pre-Socratic Philosophers* (Cambridge, 1962), pp. 320–62.

4. *Metamorphoses*, 1. 422–23; text, Loeb edition (Cambridge, Mass., 1916), 1:32.

5. Two English translations were made of Manilius's poem on world harmony in the late seventeenth century: by Edward Sherburne (London, 1675), dedicated to Charles II; and by Thomas Creech (London: J. Tonson, 1697).

6. *Virgil: A Study in Civilized Poetry* (Oxford, 1963).

7. For Pope's *Rape of the Lock* I treat certain psychological dimensions from the cards as popular emblems in "How Really to Play the Game of Ombre...," *Eighteenth Century Life*, 4 (June 1978): 104–6.

8. Cf. Earl R. Wasserman, *The Subtler Language* (Baltimore, Md., 1959).

9. *The Dialogues of Plato*, trans. B. Jowett (New York: Random House, 1937), 1:17.

10. Cf. Charles Mitchell, "Donne's 'The Ecstasy...,'" *SEL* 8 (1968): 91–101.

11. *The Works of George Herbert*, ed. F. E. Hutchinson (Oxford, 1953), pp. 41–42.

12. Ibid., p. 48.

Chapter Seven

1. "Critical Problems in Editing Herbert's *The Temple*," in *The Editor as Critic and the Critic as Editor*, papers at a Clark Library seminar, 13

Nov. 1971 (Los Angeles: University of California, 1973), pp. 3–40.

2. *The Works of George Herbert*, ed. G. E. Hutchinson (Oxford, 1953), pp. 38–39. All page references to Herbert's poems are to this edition.

3. Ms. Rawlinson, D 179, fol. 87, Bodleian Library, described by Hutchinson, p. 1vi.

4. Those who do not have access to the microfilm of the W manuscript or the facsimile edition of it by Childs and DiCesare may reconstruct the W version from Hutchinson's textual notes at the bottom of p. 66.

5. Gratitude goes to Mario DiCesare for being sufficiently persuaded by my argument on "Church-lock and key" as to have adopted (and strengthened) it in the making of his text for the Norton Critical Edition of *George Herbert and the Seventeenth Century Poets* (New York, 1978), pp. 22, 206–7.

6. I like very much Stanley Fish's *The Living Temple: George Herbert and Catechizing* (Berkeley, Cal., 1978); nevertheless I believe that to the extent that every poet is a "builder," a formalist approach still deserves a place in criticism.

Chapter Eight

1. The texts I use, incorporating references hereafter, are the facsimile of *A Modest Confutation* in W. R. Parker, *Milton's Contemporary Reputation* (Columbus, O., 1940); the *Animadversions*, ed. Rudolf Kirk and William Baker, and the *Apology*, ed. Frederick L. Taft, the two latter works in the Yale *Complete Prose Works of John Milton*, vol. 1 (New Haven, 1955).

2. J. A. Wittreich, Jr., *Achievements of the Left Hand*, ed. Michael Lieb and John Shawcross (Amherst, Mass., 1974), comes to an opposite conclusion (pp. 22–23), apparently overlooking the fact that the theatrical *persona* was originated by Milton, not by the Confutant. I believe Milton knew what he was doing: in seventeenth-century pamphleteering, as in love and war, all's fair.

3. *Works*, ed. Philip Wynter (Oxford, 1863), 9:388.

4. During his argument with Edward Coffin, S.J., on clerical marriage Hall twits the English priest on his "virginity" (*Works*, 7:497 ff.).

5. Clement Boase and W. F. Courtney, (*Bibliotheca Cornubiensis* [London, 1874–82]) as far as I know, turned Walker's report of the assize sermon into a bibliographical ghost: "*An Assize Sermon at Launceston*, 1661, 4⁰."

Chapter Nine

1. In my note, "Sir Thomas Browne's Early Reputation as a Scientist," *Seventeenth Century News* 36 (Spring 1978): 22–23, I report the existence of a manuscript translation into Danish of *Vulgar Errors* dated 1652, the earliest evidence outside England that Browne was known for scientific enquiry. The manuscript is in the University of Copenhagen Library.

2. The parenthetical documentation applies to both editions of *The Works of Sir Thomas Browne* by Geoffrey Keynes: the earlier six-volume edition (London: Faber, 1928–31), and the later four-volume edition (University of Chicago Press, 1964), vol. 2.

3. Joseph Needham, *A History of Embryology* (Cambridge, 1934), pp. 110–12; E. S. Merton, "Sir Thomas Browne's Embryological Theory," *Journal of the History of Medicine* 5 (1950): 416–21.

Chapter Ten

1. *Oraisons funèbres de Bossuet* . . . (Paris, 1851), "Essai," p. x.

2. Quoted by Barbara Kiefer Lewalski, *Donne's Anniversaries and the Poetry of Praise: The Creation of a Symbolic Mode* (Princeton, N.J., 1973), pp. 182–83.

3. *Funerals of a Right Reverend Father in God Patrick Forbes of Corse, Bishop of Aberdeen* (Aberdeen: Edward Raban, 1635).

4. *The Archbishop of Canterbury's Speech; or, His Funderal Sermon, Preacht by Himself on the Scaffold on Tower-Hill, on Friday, the 10. of Ianuarie 1644* . . .

5. (London, 1682), p. 98.

6. Preached on 12 December 1672, appended to Wilkins's *On the Principles and Duties of Natural Religion,* 6th ed. (London, 1710), pp. 1–2.

7. Wilkins, *Ecclesiastes,* ed. 1646, quoted by Charles Smyth, *The Art of Preaching* (London, 1940), p. 10.

8. John Howes, *Real Comforts* . . . *Thes. 4. 18, at the Funeral of Thomas Ball* . . . *21 June 1659,* sig. B r.

9. Cf. Nancy Lee Beaty, *The Craft of Dying: A Study in the Literary Tradition of the Ars Moriendi in England* (New Haven, 1970); and my review of it in *Renaissance Quarterly* 25 (1972): 248–49.

10. According to Congreve in the Epistle Dedicatory of his 1717 edition of Dryden's *Dramatick Works,* Dryden confessed that it was from Tillotson that he learned how to write English prose.

11. John Tillotson, *The Works,* 8th ed. (London, 1720), 1:239.

12. *Table Talk of John Selden,* ed. S. H. Reynolds (Oxford, 1892), no. 36, p. 60.

13. (London, 1680).

14. *Funerals of Bishop Forbes,* 1635, pp. 57–58.

15. *A Sermon Preached at the Funeral of That Faithful Minister of Christ Mr. John Corbet: With His True and Exemplary Character* (London, 1680), p. 72.

16. The implications of the biographical exemplum in the funeral sermon have yet to be traced as they bear on other literary genres, like the Christian elegy, the prose "character," and fiction. For biography cf. Donald Stauffer, *English Biography before 1700* (Cambridge, Mass., 1930).

In my view Stauffer overplays the encomiastic element. For fiction R. S. Crane made a beginning in "Suggestions toward a Genealogy of the 'Man of Feeling,'" *ELH* 1 (1934): 205–30.

Chapter Eleven

1. My main sources for this brief history of "original sin" are *The New Catholic Encyclopedia* (1967), the Hastings *Encyclopedia of Religion and Ethics* (1908–27); F. R. Tennant, *The Concept of Sin* (Cambridge, 1912); and Norman P. Williams, *The Idea of the Fall and Original Sin* (London, 1929).

2. Cf. P. H. Ditchfield, *The Church in the Netherlands* (London, 1893).

3. For the liberal theologians cf. Roland H. Bainton's article in *Persecution and Liberty: Essays in Honor of George Lincoln Barr* (New York, 1911), pp. 183–209; Etienne Giran, *Sébastien Castellion et la réforme calaviniste* (Haarlem and Paris, 1914), pp. 434–86; *The Writings of Arminius*, ed. W. R. Bagnall (Grand Rapids, Mich., 1956).

4. *Unum Nec.*, ed. 1655, p. 283.

5. Logan Pearsall Smith, ed. *The Golden Grove* (Oxford, 1930), p. xxviii.

Chapter Twelve

1. W. A. Greenhill, ed., *Sir Thomas Browne's Religio Medici, Letter to a Friend, & c. and Christian Morals* (London, 1881), Introduction, pp. x–xi.

2. "Sir Thomas Browne," *Macmillan's Magazine*, May 1886, p. 15.

3. Ludwig Edelstein, M.D., "The Hippocratic Oath," *Supplements to the Bulletin of the History of Medicine*, vol. 1, ed. Sigerist (Baltimore, 1943).

4. Cf. L. J. Moorman, *Tuberculosis and Genius* (Chicago, 1940), especially the cases of Marie Bashkirtseff, pp. 86 ff. and Katharine Mansfield, pp. 122–23.

5. *Religio Medici and Other Essays of Sir Thomas Browne* (London, 1892), Introduction, p. xxvi (reissued 1898).

6. *Loveday's Letters* .... London: Printed by J.G. for Nath. Brook, at the Angel in Corn-hill, 1659. All references are to this edition.

7. *University of Cambridge, Matriculation and Degrees, 544–1659* (Cambridge, 1924), pt. 1, vol. 3, p. 107. Venn's death date for Loveday, 1662, is patently wrong. The *DNB* article is sketchy.

8. Thomas Alfred Walker, *Admissions to Peterhouse, 1615–1911* (Cambridge, 1912), p. 58.

9. Tradition had it that Lazarus lived for thirty years after he was "raised" by Christ. Note brother Anthony's hint in "but half man's age" of Dante's *"nel mezzo del cammin di nostra vita."* Robert Loveday and Dr. Browne shared an enthusiasm for Dante.

10. *Annals of Nottinghamshire* (London, n.d.), 2:838.

11. *Lives of the English Poets*, ed. G. B. Hill (Oxford, 1905), 3:159.

12. On the famous air of Suffolk cf. Lord Francis Harvey, ed., *Suffolk in the Seventeenth Century* ...(London, 1902), pp. 23–24.

13. Browne had referred to the Plutarch story in *Vulgar Errors*, 7.12, so this cannot be an error.

14. Francis Blomefield, *An Essay Towards a Topographical History of the County of Norfolk*, 2nd ed., 11 vols. (London, 1805), 5:427; pedigree, 10:448.

15. *Supplement to the Suffolk Traveler*, p. 215.

16. J. Granger, *Biographical History of England*, 6 vols. (London, 1824), 5:289. The portrait forms the frontispiece to Sir John Pettus's best-known metallurgical work, *Fleta Minor* (1683).

17. *Fleta Minor*, pt. 2 of "Spagyrick Laws."

18. *N & Q*, ser. 7, vol. 4 (1887): 386.

19. Ed. 1621, pp. 248–49. Browne says, "The great Antonio was dead"; Sandys says, "The great Antonio was coming." In Ms. Sloan 1682 Browne makes the correction.

20. Norman Endicott, *UTQ* 36 (1966): 68–86. In his edition of Browne (Anchor Books, 1967), pp. 472–80, he prints the shorter version, as does L. C. Martin in the Appendix to his edition of Browne. I differed with Endicott in my review of his book in *UTQ* 4 (1968): 407–15; but we were good friends, both born in China, and both in love with Browne and good Canadian whiskey.

21. R. F. Jones, "Science and English Prose Style," *The Seventeenth Century* (Stanford, Cal., 1951), p. 93.

22. I am happy here to express publicly my gratitude to Sir Geoffrey Keynes for becoming so persuaded by this argument (and adding further evidence) as to prepare the deluxe edition of *A Letter to a Friend*, published in Boston by David R. Godine in 1971.

Chapter Fourteen

1. *Paradise Lost*, ed. A. W. Verity (London, 1910).

2. *John Milton: Paradise Lost*, ed., Merritt Y. Hughes (New York, 1935), p. 96. He corrects this view in "Milton's Limbo of Vanity," in *Th'Upright Heart and Pure*, ed. A. P. Fiore, O.F.M., Duquesne Univ. Press, 1967. Other useful studies are: E. L. Marilla, "Milton's Pardise of Fools," *English Studies* 42 (1961): 159–64; Berta Mortiz-Siebeck, "Milton's 'Paradise of Fools,'" *Anglia* 79 (1961): 153–76; and Norma Phillips, "Milton's Limbo of Vanity and Dante's Vestibule," *ELN* 3 (1966): 177–82.

3. *A Geographical Dictionary of Milton* (Ithaca, N.Y., 1919); cf. Gilbert, "Milton's China," *MLN* 26 (1911): 199–200; and Y. Z. Chang, "Why Did Milton Err on Two Chinas?" *MLR* 65 (1970): 493–98.

4. Ed. Sir George Staunton (London: Hakluyt Soc., 1853).

5. Ibid., 1:32.

6. J. J. L. Duyvendak, "Simon Stevin's Sailing Chariot," *T'oung Pao* (Leiden) 36 (1942): 401–7.

7. Ed. Meerman, 3. 23. 18–19; the poems are in *Farraginia Libera*,

156 NOTES TO PAGES 135–40

3:229–34, and *Epigrammata*, no. 22.

8. Ed. Kern, 1:95.

9. (Antwerp, 1601). Professor Charles Boxer of London has translated from the Portuguese several of the sources which Mendoza used for his history of China. I am grateful to Professor Boxer for drawing my attention to the article on Simon Stevin.

10. *The Hiero-glyphica of Horapolla Nilous*, tr. A. T. Cory (London, 1840), p. 23: "In this race of creatures there is no male . . . the eggs of the vulture that are impregnated by the wind possess a vital principle." A picture of a female vulture fertilizing her egg by wind can be seen in J. P. Valerianus, *Hieroglyphica* (Frankfort, 1678), p. 217.

11. *Pseudodoxia Epidemica*, 5.20.

Index of Names

158